Mother Homer is Dead . . .

The Frontiers of Theory

Series Editor: Martin McQuillan

Visit the Frontiers of Theory website at www.edinburghuniversitypress.com/series/tfot

Mother Homer is Dead . . .

Hélène Cixous

Translated by Peggy Kamuf

EDINBURGH
University Press

Edinburgh University Press is one of the leading university presses in the UK. We publish academic books and journals in our selected subject areas across the humanities and social sciences, combining cutting-edge scholarship with high editorial and production values to produce academic works of lasting importance. For more information visit our website: edinburghuniversitypress.com

© Hélène Cixous, *Homère est morte...*, Editions Galilée, Paris, 2014, 2020
English translation © Peggy Kamuf, 2018, 2020

Edinburgh University Press Ltd
The Tun – Holyrood Road, 12(2f) Jackson's Entry, Edinburgh EH8 8PJ

First published in hardback by Edinburgh University Press 2018

Typeset in 10.5/13 pt Sabon by
Servis Filmsetting Ltd, Stockport, Cheshire,
and printed and bound by CPI Group (UK) Ltd, Croydon, CR0 4YY

A CIP record for this book is available from the British Library

ISBN 978 1 4744 2511 7 (hardback)
ISBN 978 1 4744 2512 4 (paperback)
ISBN 978 1 4744 2513 1 (webready PDF)
ISBN 978 1 4744 2514 8 (epub)

Contents

Series Editor's Preface

Since its inception Theory has been concerned with its own limits, ends and after-life. It would be an illusion to imagine that the academy is no longer resistant to Theory but a significant consensus has been established and it can be said that Theory has now entered the mainstream of the humanities. Reaction against Theory is now a minority view and new generations of scholars have grown up with Theory. This leaves so-called Theory in an interesting position which its own procedures of auto-critique need to consider: what is the nature of this mainstream Theory and what is the relation of Theory to philosophy and the other disciplines which inform it? What is the history of its construction and what processes of amnesia and the repression of difference have taken place to establish this thing called Theory? Is Theory still the site of a more-than-critical affirmation of a negotiation with thought, which thinks thought's own limits?

'Theory' is a name that traps by an aberrant nominal effect the transformative critique which seeks to reinscribe the conditions of thought in an inaugural founding gesture that is without ground or precedent: as a 'name', a word and a concept, Theory arrests or misprisions such thinking. To imagine the frontiers of Theory is not to dismiss or to abandon Theory (on the contrary, one must always insist on the it-is-necessary of Theory even if one has given up belief in theories of all kinds). Rather, this series is concerned with the presentation of work which challenges complacency and continues the transformative work of critical thinking. It seeks to offer the very best of contemporary theoretical practice in the humanities, work which continues to push ever further the frontiers of what is accepted, including the name of Theory. In particular, it is interested in that work which involves the necessary endeavour of crossing disciplinary frontiers without dissolving the specificity of disciplines. Published by Edinburgh University Press, in the city of Enlightenment, this series promotes a certain closeness to that spirit: the continued exercise of critical thought as an attitude of inquiry which counters modes of closed or conservative opinion. In this respect the series aims to make thinking think at the frontiers of theory.

Martin McQuillan

Prologue

This book has already been written by my mother down to the last line. While I am recopying it, here it goes and writes itself otherwise, moves away despite me from the maternal nudity, loses sanctity, and we can do nothing about it.

I decided to incrust into this construction that disobeys Maman some pages drawn from her saintly simplicity. The book par excellence would be full of books and of those magical photos that one sees come to life beneath the gaze of a passionate reader, it would open onto cities that would open onto other cities where my mother stayed. Most often one sees my mother holding onto me with the one hand and her cane with the other. Her face is raised toward me, she is consulting me with a shining gaze, I am smiling at her and she believes me. I am her maternal father.

And what if she had been as tall as me? Or taller?

This is not the book I wanted to write.

I do not write it.

It is my mother who dictated it this last year (2013), without wishing to, without her wanting to, without my wanting to. This year had begun in 1910, it was immense, supertemporal, and all the while I had a premonition that she would die, before the end.

1 July: unique day among all her other days where she will have been at once dead and alive. I was holding her in an embrace forever.

It is the first July without her, no, not without Ève.

1 July something invisible, inaudible, unreadable happened between us in the bedroom.

At that moment there was not time. An interval, without measure. Without schedule. Without advent. Without ad. Right before the without ève, without event.

That's where I want to stay.

I skip.

Today is right away already 12 July 2013.

13 July 2013

'She always consoled me,' I was thinking. And now that I no longer have her body to touch, now that for twelve days she has been taken away from me as if for an excessive forever, now that she no longer lives except in the heart of my soul, now that the word 'Maman' has become timid and orphan, will she be able to console me? Fears and sorrows camp out before the gate.

And I, can I console her, as I *almost always* consoled her? The last time I said to her 'don't be afraid, my dearest', I was on all fours in front of the coffin, eleven days ago in this July of enflamed shadows, 'you are never out of my sight, my dearest', not for a thousandth of a second of this dilated time, right up until the door separates us, I have not lost a single one of your faces, in the storm of time. I gathered up each final instant, the last mouthful of water, the last word, the last kiss,[1] how would I have been able to speak today if I had not sealed the opening of your still warm lips with my lips, if I had not put my mouth on your mouth in order to taste passionately the new coldness? On the almost erased wrinkled remains of your lips.

Remain with me, remains of Maman.

I have three notebooks over which Ève reigns, the ruin, the heroine. My mother sowed them so that I would not die of her end during the first desert.

Ève never did anything on purpose. She agrees. She lets happen. She is grace itself.

These notebooks have the utility that is the virtue of my mother.

They have no other care than to accompany travellers and help one better pass away.

When Maman plagued me from February to May, saying continuously

---

1. I injected with a syringe the last mouthful of water through the crack of your partly opened mouth at 11 o'clock the night of Sunday, 30 June. You were laid out beneath the invisible slab of a heavy sleep. The last word that you hoisted out of the weight of the silence was my name, uttered two times that same Sunday around 5 o'clock in the afternoon, with a slight interval, but your voice was colourless and very distant, I could not decipher the message: was it a call for help, a complaint, a letter, I will never know. It was a word. The last days there were days without a word. Sometimes shadows of words. I said to you: I am here. At 5 o'clock the morning of 1 July, beside your bed, I said nothing, I didn't want to wake you, I watched you sleep. Note that she didn't open her eyes and yet she saw.

helpmehelpmehelpme, hundreds of times a day, when stretched out in her little boat she called for me, as I leaned over her, as close as possible, after having lowered the bars on the metal bed I said with an intensity equal to hers, 'tell me what you want me to do for you, I will do it'. And she said: 'Nothing.'

I have done these Nothings. Here they are.

The Very Long Journey: Notebooks 10–12

ATLAS
DÉPOSÉ

Accouchement

Cahier

sans

douleurs

CAHIERS NF SCOLAIRES
N° 401

The Long, very long Journey. The goal is known, but not how long the voyage is going to last, whether years, or years and years, disarmed years, it's an odyssey that will terminate not with a *nostos*, but with a descent into the subterranean cavern; or else, no, perhaps the end will be reunion? No one knows how many stops, sojourns, turnarounds await us. It will have been three years, perhaps longer, that I have been sailing along strenuously with Maman. Without the help of my guardians the notebooks, there would not have been an odyssey, but one single wailing mess. I have forgotten everything.

Every month or almost we reached another island, a new rock where some unknown evil spell awaited us. There have been so many of them – when I cast a glance at some photograph (I have never taken any, not one. The takers are my friends, my son.) a shock makes me tremble: it's the process of the infinite alteration, mutation, thus, in truth, the virulent work of death that is suddenly revealed to me. During life, leaning with my nose against Maman's face I see only her-at-the-moment, and perhaps even I see only ever the immutable, the immortal brilliance of her eyes on the alert, I grasp onto this sparkling that will never have changed at the end and I dismiss effortlessly the numerous traits that are doing the work of disfiguration. Nevertheless I obstinately took care of her appearance. Thus, with great difficulty, I transported her in 2011 to a dermatologist to clean up her face, which had been invaded like a shaggy garden of underbrush, lumps of keratitis very busy growing and proliferating. They looked like ticks. At least during the last months these parasites didn't reappear. Also the whiskers around her lips, her chin, not all of them, but those that could be pulled out. The photos leave me speechless. The immensities of the mutations, at once minuscule and brutal, have the appalling effect of the apocalypse on me. I believe and don't believe my eyes. And yet it is Ève. Ève as if bewitched, bitten. I cannot believe it. It will thus have taken centuries to hollow out, eat away, make strange, whittle down, and yet it is indeed she, dead also, it is absolutely she no change changes her, what happens to her does not happen to the absolute love I bear her and where she dwells.

I have forgotten. That is the marvellous mystery: I forget and in the forgetting are kept the traces, but torn away from their coordinates, their localisations in time. Thus in the free space of the universe the *squeak-squeak period* turns on its invisible axis. I mean a rather long sequence, weeks or months perhaps, during which, seated in her armchair (so it wasn't in 2013, the year she entered lying down), dressed, armed with books (with which I furnished her beyond all reading up until the day she stopped using her hands), she would utter a series of syllables in a single sentence squeaked out interminably.

Once I asked her if the squeak-squeak period would be over some day, but she didn't know. She had to squeak-squeak and finally I ended up becoming immune.

I note here that my feelings at the time were stamped with the natural exigency that I have always felt and that didn't leave me until January 2013 when we passed over into the last chapter. From then on I could not have *asked* anything of my mother. It was the beyond. We were no longer standing. She was lying on her back for ever, in her little boat, and I was on my knees on one side or the other and I towed through the mud of dateless time.

Entrance of Victoire

This is where the entrance of Victoire happened. Victoire was her real name. In another time, either during the life of Derrida or during the real life of Ève, I would have done poetic justice to Victoire, to her being and her name. Our doctor resembles in every way one of those flying beings who take off from Ovid, as a bird, a thrush in this case, and reach us as an aviator of flying machines in Proust, and this natural beauty that launches itself from the joy of living, I loved it all the more for being so familiar to me, and as if commanded by the joy that Maman, after having cultivated it for a hundred years, had just brutally lost. I saw Victoire as hailed by our destiny. It is as if the invisible spirit had telephoned her in her hospital office: come, come quickly to care for this old life that is no longer safe. And right away she arrives (she doesn't come, she launches herself forward) to lead with us a superexistence that is beyond us.

In the gentler times that are so near and so lost in which Ève feasted on strawberry jam like ambrosia, I would have seen Victoire as Mercury.

In these jamless times, we will always be late, Victoire and me. 'Late in relation to Ève.' The word jam makes me weep. I leave the unfinished jar in the cupboard in front of a row of Liebig soups that later I will be unable either to eat or to throw away.

According to the notebooks that the archaeologist – me – consults, The Very Long Journey would have begun with preparations on the dock at the end of 2009, the period when Ève came and dropped anchor at my house for the ultimate expedition. But one can date it to the first storms at sea where death almost carried her off, that would be in 2011. Ève believed she was dying twice, twice she announced it to me, she came to terms with it, she tells me she hopes it would happen during her sleep, it would be done during the night, without waking, stay with me, it would be sad if you were not there just on that night, I stayed, it didn't happen, she woke up, here, on the same side, with no explanation. That was good. Everything was good. Even the relief or the disappointment. It occurs to me that all this will have been a trick played by death, by its spite. Such an outcome would have been too good. The spiteful one wanted to surprise us, make us fall, slowly, make us feel its cruelty, torture us.

Remind us that it would not be content with a little snip of the scissors. It camps out in the middle of life, it seasons our dishes for years, it takes its time and mixes it with ours. I say 'death' but it's a matter of life, of life itself, of its perpetually changing its mind, of its way of giving in so as to regain its strength, of its frightened attraction for fire, of the stupefying force in its weakness. In the end you don't even know why life plays dead, perhaps because it has had enough playing with fire, it drops things for a second, sometimes it takes off again, and sometimes not. No other law except the unforeseeable. Everything rests on the instant of distraction.

The second time she didn't die was 22 April 2012. A wonderful night, I say to myself in April 2013. She was talking non-stop, I noted everything. We kept watch. I was carried away by a mystical astonishment. I was laughing. So, that was it, the Event. My mother keeps watch, foresees, keeps her eyes on the invisible, invents eschatological television, knows what she doesn't know, fends off the unforeseeable, that's her principal worry: above all she does not want to be alone for *the act with only one character*, she goes resolutely counter to Montaigne – a tranquil and solitary death, all mine, gathered up in me? No, not that! To die but not without giving you my death to live.

At midnight she calls me.

H. –Do you want to pee?

È. –That's not the question. I think I am going to die. What do I have to do?

You will come see if I am there. I'm afraid of dying and you're not there.

I feel the hour has come.

You laugh but I'm not laughing.

What are you writing?

H. –We're in extreme reporting mode.

È. –If I am dead you will not hear it.

H. –I want to hear the instant that no one hears.

È. –When it's time, it's time.

If I am going to die you are going to cry.

Look in from time to time if I am still there.
H. – But in the meantime?
È. –You don't abandon me.
I'm sorry to leave but I can't last long.
What must I do?
When it's time, it's time. You will excuse me.
H. –It's not now.
È. –It's awkward.
H. –What is?
È. –My mortal state.
All at once I'll no longer be there.
One or two more days.
I will be there or I won't be there any more.
I have to bother you some more.
Do you have a friend?
You can count on her?
It's awkward, what do you want to do?
Maybe tonight I am going to go to sleep for good.
What are you going to do tomorrow?
H. –I'm going to see the eye doctor. After, I'll stay with you.
È. –What's in the news?
H. –The elections.
È. –It's not going to be that nasty little man?
You go to sleep, maybe you don't wake up.
I hope I will still be there tomorrow.
H. –You're making me cry.
È. –One never knows.
You have always been a good little girl with me.
Maybe tomorrow morning I'm not going to wake up.
If he's elected you will tell me. We'll see.
Where are you sleeping?
One doesn't know what is happening. If it's tomorrow or today or
when. Will Pierre be there?
In any case, as for me, I don't agree with Montaigne.
If I'm lucky, I'll be there to console you.
Scratch my head.

In the morning she announces to me: 'I am dead.' I say: 'You are not
dead. For a dead woman you are very alive.'
È. –I'm exhausted. I'm half dead.
H. –We're going to catch up with the other half.
È. –We'll see.

For the first time she takes death on. She doesn't give up. She doesn't give anything up. She wants everything, on both sides.

È. –It was terrible.

H. –You fought very hard.

È. –It was not easy, I assure you. You laugh, but me …

H. –You chew. Brioche again! How about some jam? Antinightmare jam.

The tempest in *The Tempest* lasts only sixty-seven lines, for six minutes in scene 1 of act I you hear cries, goodbyes, gusts of wind. Help me! Don't leave me! What to do? You saved me. I am lost! *All lost!* I fall! *We split, we split!* Afterwards the whole play trembles and is called *The Tempest*. In the morning she is deeply asleep, she trembles less. From now on everything will happen on an island. The island is called Island of the tempest. To my surprise, upon waking, my mother, who for months has not shown a jot of interest in the century, talks about politics while polishing off a croissant.

È. –Nothing passes. Everything passes. What has not passed? Can one say that this croissant is present? In two minutes it will be no longer. Poor thing. One is never autochthonous. I never missed Algeria. It was a beautiful country. It was not our place over there. It was *a period*. Had to leave in time. Now it's the Montsouris period. Leave in time, how do you know?

–And Germany? I say.

–Germany, it was difficult to leave just like that. I had already thought about leaving. Algeria, Germany, it was not our place.

–You were useful, I say.

–Useful? For a certain time, yes. I feel sorry for people who believe. Now it's a world apart from us. I'm not nostalgic. I also lived in Strasbourg. Provisional. Everything is provisional. Arcachon was beautiful. We will go this summer. One always has several lives.

So my mother talked, resuscitated under the influence of Prospero in February 2012.

I don't know what my mother saw during that night of outbursts. According to her they took everything from her. She cried out: 'The bank!' Imperious fury: 'The bank! It must be paid!' Then I said: –I paid! *È.* –You paid? *H.* –At the bank. You needn't worry. *È.* –And the jewellery? –I'll take care of it later, I say. –Later? says my mother. Toolate!

We missed out on hope. Life leaves under our noses. –No, not toolate, I say, everything will be done. You can trust me. I said this with conviction. If she trusted me I could forcibly keep the toolate at some distance. I built frail little bridges of time, at the last minute. My mother would let me do it. She no longer believed, but if I wanted to believe, she wouldn't prevent me. She has always followed me, without any belief, in my foreign extravagances, I embark for amorous climes that she considers totally aberrant, right away she's bought her ticket. Not dying, she does that for me when she was already nearing the other shore. For me: for Maman. She makes me the mother for the dying child that she is.

I no longer know when I stopped believing myself. My notebooks know.

Late! I had said the fearful word. *Late* is the bad word of these supernumerary weeks. The time when my mother struggles day after day is a time unmasted, pierced, shaken by tempests, battered by winds, surrounded by hostile forces, she can only regret it in an apologetic voice, all the exertions she sees me do to keep her with me, she comments on them with a sorrowful Toolate! I make her ingest an antibiotic called Toolate. However she takes the Toolate as a oneneverknows. At least up until the month of May. In May she stops wanting to pay up. Paid enough! Mouth sewn shut. In June she pulls the sheet up to her chin. There is no more question.

I would have liked to insert here a chapter 'My mother and Politics': that my mother is interested in everything. In everything equally. Politics are as important and the source of feelings as the market, the style of life in Manchester with her sister, worldwide health. The universe is an ocean populated with little fish and Behemoths, in which swim her mind and her moral reflection. Eating, dying, killing, caring, aiding. First Aid, her motto. Her way of practising the culture of life. We always voted. As a modern pro-European woman, she practises all the sports as soon as they present themselves, so regularly voting, and driving the Renault. One summer she stops driving, she yields to the principle of reality, but she continues to vote and to watch over the upkeep of the car. 'Disconnect the battery before leaving.' Written with chalk on the garage door. Lay it flat to start up again. Later I will never be able to make up for her poetic inventions: Ève sees the political world with an artist's sensibility, like a child initiated into evil by Grimm's fairy tales. Do not forget that the night of 22 April 2012, when the hull of the ship was caving in, she lived her last mental hours as a citizen. In July 2012 she can only journey her life by covering one metre after another, rolled carried. However the old car works, that's good.

23 July 2013, having written these political notes I felt widowed. One discovers things while writing, as in archaeology when one digs: I

thought I was uncovering the face of my mother child. And I stumble upon a kind of intimate companion of my being in society, in the good sober sense, which is the unchangeable spokesperson of the people. It's as if I had lost the people.

Finally, it was a beautiful night.

È. –What can one do when one is so old? I am nothing any longer.

H. –At night you make a lot of noise. A lot of pee.

È. –I have nothing else to do. (*Pause*). Too bad.

Too bad, I thought. We fought the good fight side by side. In another play the daylight would have found us lying in each other's arms, I thought.

Now my mother is afraid of the night. One can't see anything. It's not very light. Here we are both of us supposing that 'It' will come at night. 'Don't give me up!' says my mother. 'Don't leave me alone!'

Now I am as afraid of the night as the day. I leave her calmly sleeping at 11 o'clock at night, I sleep at a crazy speed, at 5 o'clock I go down the little hallway, the narrow conduit populated with spectres and illusions, I murmur 'Maman', what am I saying! 'Maman' is me, if my mother still lives. It's only if I had lost my old child that 'Maman' would be the one I call for help to disinter me from this living burial.

16 July 2013

I write to console me with you. I write through you, I write what you write to me, you write me, my beloved, it's you who gives me your gentle hand that is used to my feeling, the hand that Montaigne couldn't count on, La Boétie having left before. I scratch myself with your hand precisely where it burns. I am lucky: it is not your right hand it's your left hand that had gone out of use. Write me this letter, I hope that you will still be there tomorrow in my hand.

Suddenly the idea occurs to me that, on that so sweetly glorious night of 22 April 2012, which, subsequently, I deemed to be like an adorable moment of preparation for the final act, a rough draft, an exercise that my mother had me do as if I were her firefighter and she the queen of the firemen, while waiting, when, following her uncertainty, I had not mustered all my forces, I had felt only a half-terror, that night my mother really saw the Invisible enter. Perhaps death had begun its campaign. Perhaps it had really cast its spell and we were in its swath or under its strange benevolence. Perhaps we were lodged in its hotel. Afterwards we lived in another existence, watched over by some unknown commiseration in a meagre, dilapidated reprieve, which granted us all the time necessary to disintegrate, to bring ourselves beyond regret, to the point of dried-up desire, to the point of extinction of every appetite one after the other, down to the least little need, so as to lead us to wisdom and consent and push us to the point where desire no longer desires – to the point of desiring to no longer desire desiring. There is no verb any longer. Merely the indifferent urgency to let oneself go. My mother will call this goal, in English, 'To bed.'

Between 13 January and dawn on 1 July 2013, the fight was pitiless, everything happened non-stop, at a truly mad pace, a constant high speed, quasi-motionless, in an extraterrestrial duration, like an hour stretched out over months as in a dream. And every minute of this hour was fatal. Meanwhile I *was able* to think most often that this *unheimlich* hour could last a year perhaps and sometimes longer.

14 July 2013

At 9 o'clock in the morning I go down to your room to replenish my forces there. This morning it's with the sewing box sitting in your armoire that I quenched my thirst. I opened it. It is full of your ancient hotchpotch big buttons never pointless, worn-out skeins, two thimbles, which I put on my finger to feel your finger once again, an old ceramic ring. On the outside the box is in good condition, a wise old dog that doesn't look its age. Inside it's a brain that has lost the sense of the work of time: one amasses strands of thread, pins, a fastener, bits of braid, as if one were expecting a famine. Or as if one were compulsively taking in poor orphans.

At 2 o'clock in the afternoon, thirsty for you. This time I open the third drawer of your bureau, which I had refrained from touching three days ago. It's a jumble. That's you all right: the improbable union of the shambles and the most regular order, from which is born a universe. The shambles is a disparate array of dozens of kitchen recipes cut out of magazines, not one of which ever gave results, or maybe just one. The array is congealed like the seeds of an ideal culinary workshop. You never felt the need to make it a reality. It is your Idea. On the other side of this warehouse, two large exercise notebooks, aged and childlike. On the cover you have written in very large, important letters:

Childbirth
without
pain
Cixous Ève midwife 14/10/62

Décembre 1962

cat	Nom prén	sexe	heure	N°
10	Heroriam	♂		1373
11	Bagazgaia	♂	7h	1374
12	Jemni	♂	14h	1375
14	Messaoui	♂	19h	1376
15	Berrachad	♀	7h	1377
16	Alkhelal	♂	12h	1378
16	Yacef	♂	12h	1379
16	Saadallah	♂	19.30	1380
17	Hadj Kahin	♂	17.30	1381
19	Zerrouk	♀	8.30 Lbauie	1382
19	Bourous	♂	4h	1383

cat	Nom prén	sexe	h	or	N
19	Talbi Abdi	♂	17h		1384
20	Hammoude	♀	14h		1385
21	Taoust Kara	♂	11h		1386
21	Bellili	♀	17h		1387
22	Sadaoui	♂	4h		1388
22	Medaui	♂	14h		1389
23	Benmebak	♂	20h		1390
25	Belaksaoui	♂	2h		1391
25	Kerouani	♂	14h		1392
26	Hamich Hamid	♀	18.15		1393
27	Belaid Souad	♀	18.20		1394
27	Moussaoui	♂	20h		1395

---

l'apprentissage

Acquisition du comportement qu'il
faut avoir au moment de l'acc
l'accouch. par une activité globale
toutes les fonctions y participent
techniques d'adaptation a l'A

A quoi sert cette préparation?
Acc = E.   Il y a des gens qui
sont en écriture pas. Nous nous
également des preuves. Il y a des
mauvais qui croient que cette
méthode atténue. C'est faux. Nous
allons indolores. La douleur
n'est pas fatale pas nécessaire,
n'utile? (une lettre d'invitation
qui veut souffrir).

A.s.d c'est la cause tout dou-
loureuse, mais on se sent accou-
cher. Vous aurez des sensations
renouvelées du début à la fin.
Un muscle aussi important que
la matrice a des liaisons avec le
corps.

Notion d'effort
Ce n'est pas question de hasard.
A de preuves. Celle qui se prépare
bien réussit bien, mais celle
qui ne fait pas d'efforts, ne peut
pas acc. il faut se préparer,
prendre des cours, les relire
et suivre les cours. Vous devez
mettre l'enfant au monde dans les
meilleures conditions. La douleur
est une mauvaise condition.

A la fin de la préparation
vous allez vous trouver devant
l'acc. On vous donne la possi-
bilité de dirigier l'acc. Il part-
icipation est active. Il y a une
normalisation de l'A. A ser.
plus rapide c'est important pour
l'enfant. Pourquoi liberté, toute
la vie de l'enfant en dépend.
La douleur   La douleur d'où vient
qu'est elle? Un phénomène nerveux

La théorie continue visverale en mécanique

Mécanique ondulatoire ou quantique
Travaux Pan
Théorie

Rapport. Corps-Aire (expérience)
Aboutir était expér- mode de vie
actions reliées —
On abandonne les mystères de tahument
2 grands théorist expliquant
— Hier- populant (Freud) analyse
Tout à bien phynologique (Parlov)
appelanalyse- vague- avec connaît.
ligne
Parlow- expériences et observ. ont
fait définir des règles
vation fondamentale : condi-
tionnement.

théorie l'action de nerveux expérieux.
Parlow dot que les force point où pas
s'étendu similitation. Autoperiorit
à l'extendre-

Look: two philosophical beauties, a hundred pages of illustrated, patient, scientific analyses, composed in a strong, harmonious handwriting that breathes deeply, a performative masterpiece, where you can't tell who sees things through better or best. The notebook itself is born of a successful childbirth.

I spill a flood of ideas like tears:
–how one sees from the layout of the pages the mental force, and thus, reciprocally, the manual force of my midwife mother
–how she was a midwife par excellence until the day, two or three years ago, when she ceased being one. That was long ago. Everything has become long ago
–there was in these notebooks everything we needed to save us from the abyss. If only we had had them! during the labour! Those months of mortal pregnancy, that terminal childbirth, poorly attended, the maladjusted, misunderstood pain. These flexible responses, these sensible reflections on the variations in anxiety, contractions, pain, these graduations in activity, consent, this listening to the egos engaged in a fight for life life victory, all this judicious advice that we did not follow, these recipes for rejoicing in the midst of danger, this spiritual treasure, these magical weapons, this golden tunic ordered by Thetys from Vulcan that would have made us almost totally invincible, except for the heel. Except for the heel. My mother lost the midwife in person around 2010. At a hundred years old it no longer interests her. She lets in the child who was feebly lurking at her door. The metamorphosis is progressive, cunning, rapid. It begins with the voice and progresses to all the limbs. On 13 January 2013 she complains of a violent pain in her right foot. I didn't see anything. My foot hurts. I felt the toes, the sole. Maman's wide, solid foot. On 14 January a mass of blackish blood formed an enormous pocket beneath the heel. What's the matter with my foot? At the end there was nothing left of the midwife except a furiously giant force in her hands. Thereafter all my mother's strength resides in her fist. Her legs dangle. Her hands do not give up. They testify to the greatness that was until Sunday, 30 June. In those hands hundreds of newborn heads left the trace of their passage through the strait that leads to the light. The muscles of the fingers do not forget. The legs hang loose.

At the end I can no longer touch anything but Maman's head I feel her temples that are hollowing out beneath the sad caress of my index finger, then I slide my fingers on her skull in her strong white hair, at the end only Maman's head accepts being touched, I slide my fingers among all the fires that devour her skin. At the end only Maman's head resists the fire. She keeps her head emerged above the disaster, her eaten-up bloody body hidden beneath the sheet that she defends tooth and nail.

At the end she is dressed in nothing but a half-pyjama slipped only over her chest, the army of wounds advances over the old terrain, the fabric falls back, the skin blisters and comes off.

I examine the top of her withered thighs, I'm looking for a few square centimetres still fit to receive the shot of calciparine. There is less and less of it. I have to attack her to defend her. One can rely for the strike only on this brief part of the body. How far will we go, how far, for how long this pharmakonnery, and with each shot I lose and I gain a little bit of skin a little bit of blood. We don't have many provisions left. We lower our heads, we advance on the path that goes up while going down, centimetre after centimetre. When we reach the summit – then – then?

Opening her drawers, one will easily find hundreds of cooking recipes. My mother links a certain number of arts and sciences whose metonymic flux is nothing other than a fabulous recipe for worldwide human life. The worldwide human being lives in several countries, has a nearly unlimited curiosity, the soul of a traveller from the beginning of the nineteenth century, doesn't hesitate to leave for Marseille or Hamburg toward diverse Orients, she would go as far as India if she had the time for it, wants to taste anything and everything, experiences a modest and clear sensual delight at the thought of doing the Himalayas, what she regrets is having missed the chance of Easter Island when she was in Chile. She missed those three days. My mother was born to explore. Any means are good for a trip.

At ninety-five years old in 2005 she stops taking plane trips except with me. For the distant places she takes the television. She goes all over the world, herself alone both public and coryphæus. Around her, Humanity expresses itself in her voice, a Humanity who in her play is optimist, reasonably. 'They showed us these men', she says, 'in the Himalayas, the paths climb up, descend . . .'

en avant : vessie et méat
en arrière : utérus : le corps et le col
un muscle creux. 2 orifices
interne et externe. Le col débouche
dans le vagin dont il en fait externe
s'appelle la vulve.

au avant : vulve. Le tout c'est le
périnée.

Le corps de l'utérus se développe.
Le col pas au moment de la
grossesse.

œuf 12 cellules

ovaire

Ovulation

amarres : les ovaires plat ovale

---

des phrase.

le plancher au dessus

Fond. G. l'U. pénètre dans la
cavité abdominale.

A. dans le détroit inférieur.

2. la peau distendue et colorée
suit le mouvement et se cambre
sous la peau du ventre. La sangle
abdominale, en se contractant
exerce une pression sur l'utérus.
Éducation musculaire. Au repos
les muscles qui ne sont pas de rapport.

L'utérus s'arrête à la cage tho-
racique. Le diaphragme : muscle
de la respiration. Exerce une action
sur l'utérus. Ici + action rapport
par la respiration.

---

perception.
Poche eaux. Rupture membranes. Infec-
tion en rapport avec milieu extérieur.
Sécurité de l'échange. Après 1 jour
rupture, il faut déclencher A.

Contractions : de travail
Repos. - intensité croissante.
Durée + +
Intervalles - -

intervalles
15 à 60 s

35 - 45"   4 à 5 55"   55 à 60"

effacement   5 à 6 à   5 à 6 à
s'orifice   8 à 10   Dil. Complète
dilaté

sensat.   sensat.   sensat.
larges   + +   + + +
y répondre différemment

DPossible intensité on peut se pas être

---

d'accord. Il y a une petite sensation qui
donne une hache. Il ne faut pas y
penser. Il faut s'occuper. Aller lire
des mais .... Au moment de la
contraction. échanges respiratoires se
relaxer que si sait inviter à
contract. 2 respir. puis se relâcher
après contract. encore 3 échanges
pour être bien oxygéné. Le cerveau
ou de dormir. C'est un travail intel-
lectuel et sensation de repos. Dès qu'on
se réveille, échanger, ensuite se ren-
dormir. Meilleur relaxer pour être
en forme.

Dilatation 2e partie. Maintenant sensation +
nette, partant au dessus du pubis et
qui partent en ondes en haut de
l'U. Suivez la montée et la des-
cente. Les contract. appuient la
présentation devant elle.

Pendant ces contract. sensat. + fortes.
Maintenant avoir une activité
plus importante. Avoir des échanges

The Beautiful Summer of 2011

She called me constantly, all the time she wasn't sleeping, she called me,
then she meowed wah wah, she hammered, to change tortures we do
exercises. Let's do multiplications: H. −2 times 2. È. −4. H. −Good. 2
times 5? È. −8. H. Division: 20 by 2. È. −10. H. −3 times 5? È. −? H. 5
times 3? È. −15.

She grabs me by the right arm: −Where are you? H. −Where am I?
È. −You're far away. You're taking the boat. I'm alone. Hélène! H. −I'm
sitting a metre away from you. I'll come closer. And now? È. −No. Are
you coming closer? H. −I'm fifty centimetres away. È. −Where are you?
It's a matter of coming closer internally, internal to solitude. È. −Wah,
wah wahm. H. −How many times a day do you meow? Ève, with large
brown eyes. *−Many −Far too many. I do what I can. That's good. H. −*
What is the word *you say most often? È. −That's* good. *H. −You do good*
work, Maman. È. −You see?! H. −Now I am going to work. È. −Shame.
Rhymes with lame. Wah mwah wahm. You're leaving? H. −No, I'm
right close by. È. −It's not far?

In bed, that night. È. −I am lost. H. −Where? In a city? In a forest?
È. −In a forest. Can you help me? H. −Do what? È. − I have to come
back. H. −Take my hand. Follow me. È. −Out! Everything is outside.
Far. Difficult.

È. −My head is far. Me, I am lost. What can be done with me? With
old people like that. I found you again, my little darling you. My head
is far. H. −We'll wait for it. In what city are we? È. −It's Berlin, no? No,
it's not Berlin? H. −No. Have you already lived in Berlin? È. −No. What
city is it?

Elsewhere. È. −Don't forget me. H. −I'm here. È. −You are here and I
am elsewhere.

È. −Help me. How do I get out of here? H. −What do you want? È.
−I want to become like everyone else. Help me. I want to get out of this
state.

One day she reads passionately The Boy Who Wanted to Sleep. *Her way of reading: she follows every word step by step. I see that the words march by slowly in front of her, wait for her. For hours. A patience of which I have only a used-up remnant. The book lends itself without complaining to her going back over and over again. Sometimes she spends a day ruminating in the meadow of a page, grazes the Hebrew of the text, bewitched by the arabesques of the letters. I guess that the book chants to her a lullaby of love. She is reading? asks a passer-by. The book holds her hands. Listens to her groaning. She repeats: me too I would like to sleep. −Why? −Because it's a grey day.*

But in that year 2011, she cries out. She is still very far from sleep. The torpor will envelop her only starting on 13 January 2013.

'Who are you?'
It's the eve of her a hundred and first birthday. Ève is resplendent. She eats a brioche, which is the breast and life. Whimpers. Meows. Redoes the creation of the world. Here is the cat. Ève. −That's the cat. Does it have a name? Isn't it Roro. She tries out all the pawns she has at her disposal. H. −No. It's Philia. What is the name of P.-F.'s son? È. −Don't know. Philio? H. −What is your mother's name? È. −Hélène. That's not it? (She looks at me with her round, shining, light brown eyes.) H. −If you wish. But your mother in the past? È. −Omi! (She thinks. Suddenly her sister comes back.) Where is Éri? H. −She has left. Ève frightened. − Left? Where? H. −She is dead. È. −What! Éri is dead? H. −Five years ago already. She told you on the phone that she had had enough. She said 'J'en ai marre' in French. You said to her: so leave. Ève frightened. −Éri is dead! She eats her brioche. Life remains. Ève, her mouth full. −Who are you? H. −I don't know. Tell me. È. −Isn't it Hélène? (Eyes wide with alarm.) H. −You are sure? È. −You are Hélène. H. −And who is Hélène? È. −My daughter. (A bite of brioche to think with.) You are my father and my mother. What are you writing? H. −Your name: È,V,E. It's a pretty name. È. −Yes, the name *is beautiful. Are you the one who chose it? H. −Yes, my daughter, I'm the one who chose it. È. −That's good.*

The brioche is a nice big breast, she's not afraid of it. A love for the brioche that doesn't eat her, that she eats, has come to her. A love for Roro blossoms. Roro is a brioche that laughs.

Ève to Roro. −Why are you so fat? You have fat tits. Roro. −Do you want me to give you a little of them? Ève (modest). −Alittle.

Thereafter every morning at 8 o'clock, during the two years before the battle of January 2013, Ève leans her forehead against Roro's fat tits.

The brioche is an edible shield. Ève has a natural compassion for the weak who suffer and tremble like her. (A noise.) È. −Uh oh! What is that noise? I'm afraid. It's too much! H. *–Someone is peeling carrots.* È. *–Poor carrots! Ohhhh! It frightens me!* H. *–Are you afraid you'll be eaten?* È. *–Yes, yes. (She chews her brioche. Casts a glance. Says: 'Frightened!' She swallows.) Oh! I'm frightened. Who is it?* H. *–The door to the kitchen.* È. *–Oh! Okay! it's not serious.*

I place myself perpendicularly to Ève lying on the couch in my bedroom. She whimpers, wahwahs, cries out in my direction, squalls of complaints, cries out my name, protests, ich bin verloren, *I am lost, my backside hurts, I rise slide an anti-bedsore cushion under her backside, sit down again, you are far away, where are you? I rise, a small feeling of resentment rises, a snake crawls from the couch to the armchair, hisses, twists itself, enough! I've had enough, says one of them, enough, says the other, the armchair hisses, the couch crawls. I change rooms. From here I can barely hear her, I wait, a phone call from the theatre. I hear her. I listen. Flogged prayer. I revort. That's a comic revolt that comes to me from Henry Brulard. It flogs me. Angry thoughts. –Enough! –Enough! Over there Maman moans. Little blows of a plaintive hammer on the eardrums. Torture. Pause. Phantom complaints. Wahwah. Where are you? Tick-tock of complaint. I time it. Sixty moans a minute. The mechanical lapidation of the eardrums. –Can you restrain yourself, my little hammer? –No. –So, change? For example: sing. –Can't.*

After three months of wahwahing I adapt.

Here, the first page of the white Matisse notebook, it is 7 o'clock in the morning on Friday, 25 January 2013, an innocent date. And yet since Sunday, 13 January, the days have had a very strong personality. They are like subchapters in the *Odyssey*. Yesterday a beautiful article by Loret in *Libé* a full-page capital-letters Dead, Carlos Fuentes, H.C., headline that 'in the past' would have given me pleasure, but leaning over the cradle grave, once again I looked at life's mockery: one does not witness one's own success. That is even the law in literature, at least for me. Already in '69 when I received the Medicis prize, which delighted Carlos from a distance, I was not there, I had descended, precisely, into Hades. There is in 'the theatre of the world' a life of mine that takes care of its/my business, while the Hélène-soul toils in the twisted furrow of mortality

All of this written with the accompaniment of Ève's threnody help-meeehelpmeee since 5 o'clock in the morning.

At 4 o'clock, in the night populated by the vigours of the cats who come and go, I had decided to give her death. At 4 o'clock. This was happening in the present. Two hours ago of this page it was the present or the future. I rose. I had a long non-violent discussion with myself. For witnesses I had the gigantic raw red wounds on Maman's legs. Dimension: the palm of my hand. Top of the left leg, then beneath the knees two large pockets like mad eggs, trickles of blood clot, trickles of blood ooze. Beneath the right leg blackish oozing lake. Large black mass beneath the right heel. Consequence: Ève can no longer stand. Cannot bear any contact. Spent the day legs uncovered, two red blankets on the torso, rolled cushions beneath the ankles, we tinker body pieces.

On the comical side, I shiver covered in three undershirts, sweater, fleece jacket 1, fleece jacket 2, cap, but the cold is lodged in the marrows of my soul.

Attempts to find the exits: there are two? More than two?

This thought (to give her death) has one performance. It lasts four metres, the length of the hallway that carries me in a dream to her room. I slide into her bed on the armoire side, I take her in my arms I tell her my love and she rests. There are no details. Merely the beginning of a sensation of gratitude. I enter into reality that cries out its agonising salute, helpmeehelpmee the unflagging cry of the rooster whose throat is slit. If I could lift Maman, if I had arms thick with muscles, the back of a man, put her on the toilet-chair, but this traction takes two. Sitting on the toilet-chair I wait for Roro's arrival, I have but one desire: sleep, Maman, sleep, escape the pain by that good thing granted to poor mortals, sleep, hide beneath the sheet let's leave, Maman, I say in silence beneath the sheet, don't be afraid, go to sleep and don't wake up I'll keep you in my arms until fear falls asleep. Don't worry about the green beans, I'll do them myself, don't fear that I am afraid, everything's fine, let's spend our last night together, it will be like the enormous *café liégeois* on 12 August, you remember, I held the large black glass close enough to your chin and you lifted the long spoon loaded down with whipped cream, one hour after another, you had a drop on your nose, I wipe it off right before it falls in the cream, up to the last spoonful of the hour, sleep my love, I'm holding the large glass. It's long this glass, and then she rests.

One takes her beneath the arms while passing her two arms that I raise and secure around Roro's large neck, and at the same moment I take her feet at the ankles and we pivot her into a sitting position then a third of a turn, I push the toilet-chair toward her bottom, in a second I lower the special pants. Sometimes I have to convince her body to let itself bend, when a terrified tightness freezes her like a bloody stone column. This exercise is repeated four times a day. It's Roro and I who are best coordinated. I don't have strength but I have speed and the sense of the right gesture. While I detach the soiled pants in less than a second, Ève's head leans on Roro's shoulder. During the exercise Ève moans very loud tobedtobedtobed. We hurt her to avoid the worst, an extension of the bedsores. The bedsore, I can't get used to it, is the eye of the one-eyed Cyclops, that great purplish hole that foams while saying: you are warned, I will kill you. The monsters arrive quickly. The vultures precede us. We live overflown by these great patient turkeys.

I will never forget the *café liégeois* at the brasserie du Soleil. I will never forget that my mother would never forget the cauliflower from Lautaret. It occurs to me that the enormous cabbage of ice cream and whipped cream will have been the ultimate edition of the unforgettable vegetable – there must come together many conditions whose rare, random, thus supernatural conjunction calls up in us the state of exaltation that Stendhal will have achieved at the Saint Bernard pass. When I reread this moment when Henry is in the nearest approach to *perfect happiness*, I recognise the transport we feel the day of the *café liégeois* at the table near the window beneath the canopy of the mulberry tree. For such a moment one must have had the trouble of having *lived* each one as he or she can the hundred and one years of my mother. Stendhal needs twenty pages and several days with his heart pounding to report as precisely as possible the elements that crowd toward the making of the Saint Bernard event. This is the high genetic region of miracles.

If I had the time I could trace along thousands of threads back to the foot of Strasbourg cathedral where everything *really* began, probably between 1910 (Ève's birth) and 1916 (death in the Belorussian winter of her father Michael Klein). I could prove that this lump of ice cream and snowy cream is the effigy of this father for whom she was hungry and whose presence she called for during the year 2012. She needed his body, in the end. But I don't have time.

At the Soleil, Ève was physically an old fossil, she couldn't take two steps without looking as if she was going to fall, morally she had the courage that she got from her father, we kept going beyond her strength, or Eric would hold her up, raise her in the air, I would slide a folding stool beneath her bottom, she would catch her breath, we would start again, finally after twenty zigzags that multiplied the distance from the car to the terrace, we're at the table and can see in the distance the Image of the Bay with its sailing boats immobilised by the souvenir snapshot. The boats don't interest Ève: those are Faraway beings. Beneath her nose a snow more powerful than the promise of the Ocean holds all her passion. She climbs the ice cream summit, I follow her with my eyes I see myself contemplating her studious, laborious air as she plants the spoon at the right spot, raises, brings to her mouth, concentrated, her big wide hands in the centre on the right my little slender hands, the climbers are roped together, at the bottom Eric's two little girls watch with diminishing hope for signs of satiation of the old dominant cat but Ève does not put down the spoon until the last mouthful.

23 July 2013

That July the *Café Liégeois* took on extranatural dimensions. On 1 July it suddenly became the Last of the *Cafés Liégeois*. It exists in my interior storehouse like an event framed by sparklings like a painting of Jan Van Eyck where all the details are enlivened by a passionate gaze. There also exists a video of two immortal minutes on this subject. Later there will be in my consecrated memory no archive, no document more profoundly moving than this instant of grandiose innocence, and whose naïve and intense construction, almond-shaped, with at its heart my-mother-with-ice-cream and in the predellas all the angels fascinated by the little celebration, is a masterpiece. I myself leaning on my elbows at her side contemplate the ascension of the *café liégeois* while savouring each spoonful of this dazzling moment of intense pleasure. I see myself happy for this appetite free from the chains of very advanced age, delighted by Ève's *tour de force*, impressed by the spiritual resources of this fondness for food, which granted my mother a totally incalculable triumph. It is the summer of the *Café Liégeois*. Thereafter all one has to do is take up again the pages on the Saint Bernard pass, it's exactly that, the sublime, the minuscule, the mental exaltation at the altitude of 2,491 metres above sea level, the sweet feeling that one can no longer complain about destiny, that a little bit of ice cream in abundant quantity swallowed with pleasure by a semi-mouldy one-hundred-and-one-year-old being and the impression of greatness is granted to us.

Sunday, 21 July 2013, some thoughts pass by on the side of the balcony – it is too hot for her, last year it was too cold, I would wrap her up, add her tartan throw to her parka, she doesn't hear the crickets, doesn't see the fat squirrel, I tell her that he chirps like her, today is the third Sunday following the sad and splendid last Sunday of our life, an immense Sunday both seeing and blind. In my notebook that Sunday, 30 June 2013, is titled: 'Ève grows larger.' These thoughts and a hundred others pass by barefoot and dissipate in the east without my holding them back. I am totally absorbed in enjoying with my whole body a brief and perfect vision: Maman climbs the staircase that links her floor to mine, cracks open the door of my study where I am writing hunched over my field of papers, under the same desk lamp that is lit in all seasons, and holds out a tray on which she has arranged a little bowl with two slices of tomato and three radishes, a crust of the day's baguette and some *café au lait*. Raspberries. We smile at each other. She goes back down. It is noon, a Sunday in August 2000. The scene is clear, brightly coloured like a Bonnard in Arcachon, it lasts a minute, it has the charm of a video whose briefness and absence of effects assure the truth of life itself, I play it for myself several times, and the angelic friction of this little message awakens in my heart a shiver of happiness. I note it down quickly before nothingness cancels it forever. Thus this Sunday without her I am not without her. I have the power. I have her power. She made me a power. I see the paper, and in her writing so like her large hands and feet, square, firm, she has traced the words: I give power to my daughter Hélène Cixous signed Ève Cixous.

I continue on the cruel path of 25 January 2013

Ève has not eaten since 14 January. Diet: a coffee-cup of soup per day, a litre of water. She's holding out on the reserves of the human species? How long without food? Total for the week: a little tea cake, a coffee-cup of compote.

Five o'clock in the morning. I pass by. I'm wearing the ugly-bathrobe full of holes made of wool from the Pyrenees which I could never give up because Ève gave it to me forty years ago. The Ugly-Bathrobe is a familiar character for those close to me. I love it for being so naturally ugly. Ariane improvised her gibe: But-who-gave-you-that-ugly-bathrobe?

My sacred armour. H. goes forward. Hypothesis: sleeping? Dead? No. Salvation: 'Hélène! help me!' The scenario explodes noiselessly, a bubble no more consistent than some dream mist.

Sitting beside this lapidated, stained body of colossal force. Death? Has not the beginning of authority over this life. It is life that derails, leaks, soils, smears

Frequent revisiting: when Ève tells me (it was fifteen, maybe twenty years ago) the end of Omi (her mother) thirty-seven years ago. Omi Rosi Klein ninety-five years old. Fractured hip. Ève then in my place. Omi asks her sovereign daughter for help. Omi says: do it and don't tell me. Or else: give me something and don't tell me. Or else: don't tell me, do. Ève doesn't do. Says: I was afraid that it would be a comfort to me. Do. The word do. Its equivocal glimmers. Ève does not do. Perhaps Omi believes that Ève does? Same scene, otherwise: Ève says: Help me. H. –How can I help you? Tell me. È. –I don't know. Helpmeeehelpmeee. Ève a hundred and three years old. H. –Do you want some medicine? *Ève, greedily.* –Yes. I give her half a Xanax. Èveomi? I don't know. Ève believes. I don't know what she believes.

In these scenes, the mother is the daughter, we are reversed, the one who was the mother is the child, the daughter is the mother who is still the daughter, the mother is the daughter, we are born in reverse, the mother calls her mother the daughter, the daughter is the mother with milkless love, the mother to the bloodied mother, the mother all love without light, the mother without response, without being able to caress, I cannot touch Maman, the daughter is the mother whose hands are gagged, leaving the voice, the thin thread, Iamhere my love Iamhere, a meagre I'mhere that is tenuous tenacious sad, malnourished.

Saturday, 26 January 2013, I talk about the faceless hidden future, with my daughter Anne. I no longer have *any memory* of having thought of death. Only the notebook knows and tells me that Sunday the 27th black dawn, at 6 o'clock. Thus on Saturday, one day later, in thought, to have given her death, I find myself *wholly on the side of life*. I want what she wants, I say to Anne. I cannot not, I follow her. Anne thinks: but do you know what she wants? Does she want what she wants? Does she want what you want? Does she want you to want what she wants? Does she want what she doesn't know you want? I mean: does she want to know, not know, what she would like you to think that she wants, in her place? My daughter thinks thinks and doesn't tell me. At that moment I have not yet begun to think that a little bit of mother enters into the composition of my daughter, but I sense like a clue a substance as fine as some mother's wing powder spread, fine powder of the maternal, over the wounds that we share.

'She does not give me her death,' I say to my daughter.

She is the only one to whom I can say everything. Hearing myself think that I am sad: that's the very thing that I have always known, lived, received from my mother. Sad worried joy. Now I say, gripped with fright, I can no longer say everything to my mother, that is what is happening to me, I could but I cannot, a thin and sad fear of taking away from her a narrow touch of her freedom in the state of extraordinary weakness where she is damaged in a part of herself holds me back, creates blanks in my speech. Right away I bitterly reproach myself for this fear but I cannot ask my mother if I can dismiss it for she no longer responds. Except with a Yes or a No, uprooted, unfathomable syllable.

Wants
Do
Yes, no.
Yes is said for no.

Certain words have suddenly taken on the dangerous charge of a medication. They are doses. They can turn to poison according to the intensity of the interpretation.

Ève, tribute to a life in shreds

Still Saturday, 26 January, I pass on toward the bedroom. In the hallway *What If* is waiting for me, the thought of the surprise, it dissipates as I continue on my way. Ève is breathing heavily. Monumental. In the hallway *What If* is laughing in a low voice. I get up at 3 o'clock in the morning. I am sleeping very little, working around the theme 'medicalised bed'. This theme was presented yesterday with the light discretion of a duvet by Victoire. Victoire has premonitions. I pick up the expression 'medicalised bed' with tweezers. Vision: the bed of Gregor Samsa. Medicalisedbed, a toothed, hooked word. It enters, all at once the word is in the house. Medicalisedbed says: Ève is not getting up. It says, malignly: Ève will not get up. This is how I learn that until now I must have been imagining that Ève was going to get up. I write these notes with my left hand on the forehead of the page and Philia's cheek against the back of my hand. In the distance, phantom of call from my mother 'Where is the cat?' goes further away. Finished with the cats. As if Medicalised bed were an anticat.

To my children I say: 'ordeal'. Ordeal testing the human being as patience. Obviously patience as measured only at its limit. There is no patience. So long as there is some there is none. With Maman's impatience and mine we put together a kind of bandage of patience.

Perfusion of iron: I become Ève, it's stronger than me, heart and mind fixed upon the tube and bottle of black liquid. More than half an hour. A liquid à la Poe. Drop by drop Ève protests. Iron, iron. One thought among a hundred: the paradoxical work of medicine and of me: we give Ève weapons to fight us. It is *she* who must die, or live, live die, make the choice, do the work. Her freedom.

A clear message, emitted by Omi, Help me = kill me. Here, cloudy message.

I have entered into the weary region. My own interests heave a sigh: desire to live (live? there are so many kinds), that is live-move, live-work, live-banalities. But not very strong. Neither timidly, nor fierce. Getting by. Very strong: the internal appeal from Maman. All day I run toward her, stopwatched, female, bird that brought into the world an old and invalid fledgling. However this night the idea occurs to me that I want an answer to the battle by the end of 2013.

Ève has to win it.

Hidden: what awaits me 'after' Ève, if 'after' has any meaning. Hypotheses: 1) there is no after, she would remain, eternally, mixed up with me; 2) a hole in my side, or in my back, a terror. An amputation of the brain. Instead of reunion with me an immense weakening of the heart and the head, a stultifying, loss of my force of analysis

References:

1) When the little one departed in September 2005 I lost half of my brain, of my judgment, I lost the life of my interior life, armour, lance, invincibility, Thursday, 12 August, we kissed each other on the lips, at the parting, with people all around, a furtive, total, chaste kiss. He blessed me, he put his hand on my head, he quickly picked a Virginia creeper leaf that I put in my jacket pocket, he walks while staggering with pain. I say: I need your life, I need you to live. He says: me too. That means: I need me in order to live. I am exhausted. I sit down on the sofa next to Maman. I need to catch my breath, strength, cats, Maman. I say: 'Maman'. She says: 'yes, my daughter'.

2) When Papa was taken from beneath our eyes by an invisible fist, from one instant to another, I was standing, outside, I saw nothing, I had nothing, neither world, nor earth, nor time, nor tomorrow, Maman wasn't there, the world torn away and transformed into a war of annihilation, I didn't get over it until the coming of the little one.

3) What is Ève as strength-help-light for me? Divine simplicity. Without shadow, without meanness, pure fidelity, without trembling. Her present wreck without any impurity. Her cry: 'Hélène!' Her confident way of hailing. Her economy: in a word her world.

4) 1 December 2010. It has been more than a year since Ève is no longer *chez* Ève. She takes her breakfast beneath my roof. H. enters: '*È.* –Ah! The big boss. *H.* –I come to catch my breath (I've been writing since 5 o'clock in the morning). *È.* –You're right. I need it, your breath. Given that I'm already breathing from the last hole. *H.* –What is the last hole? *È.* –I don't know. You don't know the last hole so long as you haven't had it.

This year 2013 we are in the last hole. I had not expected that it would be so vast, so torturous, so Antarctic. It's been at least three years, perhaps four since we began the exploration of the last hole. The hole resembles the subterranean odyssey, it extends into labyrinths, car parks as large as engulfed cities, and since the sailors are slow, half-paralysed pushed in a wheelchair, it's an endless voyage. So long that one often forgets the goal, one believes one is making a superhuman crossing, fortunately. Thus one might be repeating the last act for several years! Maman has been on the platform with her suitcase for such a long time. A year ago she was ready for departure. Her sole fear was that I would miss the departure. She cried out as soon as I moved away from the train compartment. As the months went by, she ended up forgetting the idea of departure. She doesn't know any longer what she's doing in this train. All of her anxiety is now employed wondering what she is doing there. The platform filled up with fog. Maman looks like a surveyor. It's stifling. All the same one wants an answer because the idea that there is none is unliveable for a human being. Sometimes people depart. At least the departure is announced. Okay, this time we're going to depart. Naturally I am absent precisely for the day. This happens only once a month. Maman waits for me, I see her via telepathy, she is sitting on her bed, it's Maman with her hair dyed, the one who in the past at 8 o'clock in the morning would accompany me in the car to the seminar and then drive home alone. It's urgent. What a terrible return trip. One hurries up while begging death to wait for us. I am all alone, I got on the road taking maximum risk, my very powerful car doesn't go fast enough, time overtakes it, it is already 6 o'clock in the evening, night is going to fall on us, when I get lost. That is my fate. I enter a miserable village where the road disappears, I turn in a circle in the ruts, I ask passers-by for directions, they laugh at me, I plunge at full speed into the obscure bowels of a tunnel and I go into reverse, *I am lost*, I act out in reality the terror that haunts Ève and makes her moan all day long, *I am lost, ich bin verloren*, with what suffering we drive on astray? Night looms, I will not arrive to help my mother who is all alone, it will be too dark for me to drive. But here it happens that my daughter is lodging in just this unknown province where she teaches. And here are my dear friends Eric and Ashley. I ask them to accompany me, Maman is waiting for me at death. But no. I have already been accompanied on the trip out. They smile and say nothing. I plead in vain. I understand that death is just this. It is not at all what one thinks. It's: In Vain. It's the missed moment. One doesn't arrive there. Finally I go to my daughter's house. She tells me she is not able to accompany me. This is what Montaigne says. It's when all of a sudden those who accompany us *are not able*. There is a stop of the road, the earth, movement. I ought to spend the night at my daughter's, leave at dawn. Warn Maman. Or risk taking the dark road from which no traveller returns, while driving two hundred kilometres an hour. My daughter is lodging in a rented hangar, the floor is made of sand, I could sleep on the ground. Poor conditions of a teacher's life, but she doesn't complain. I left too late. I see now the image of Maman sitting, waiting for me. The pain I feel at this moment will never be extinguished. Alone she is over there alone here I am. I ask for a stop to time. In the past Maman would have been her own midwife, but since she has become little three years ago, she balks.

I'm sitting beside the bed. On the road that separates us I drive at all my possible speeds to arrive to help her without managing to reduce the distance. I come across no one else. It's a one-person road. Who would have believed there were so many hundreds of kilometres in these twenty centimetres. She is encircled by the Distant, the distant plants its stakes around her.

Since 13 January I have been running, I hurry, I look at my watch, I come back without losing a second, when I am going to do my seminar once a month, I leave ten minutes before the end, I cut off my speech, I leave without saying goodbye, I slip into the fear that I had taken off upon arriving.

One runs. –With whom are you racing? –I don't know. The adversary is hidden and innumerable. Death is an army. A chance in ten thousand of arriving at the same time it does? In a hundred thousand. One cannot not try to arrive before its instant. It has at its disposal regiments of illusions and imminences around my existence, among which is hidden the prize.

But well before 13 January 2013 we were in a state of war. The third Great War of my mother had begun, but no one knew when or in what city, it was insidious I didn't believe it, I was on watch out of superstition, admiration, statistics, there are not many centenarians, everything is going all right, we do Father Christmas in 2011 she has passed her hundred and one years, I costume her as December, she enters the family in red, leaning on Anne and her cane, made terribly proud by her long beard of cotton. In the days that follow she calls for her beard. She's afraid for her appendage. My beard! You're not going to throw it out! Poor beard! I put her beard away in her drawer of animated things. It is next to the tiny knitted bear that I had brought her back from London and on which she conferred the status of abandoned child. She puts it on her chest. Ève is a hospitable old giant.

At the beginning the war manifested beneath a deceptive, reassuring mask. My giant will never have been as naturally and joyfully a member of Childhood. Children recognise her as one of their own. The perspicacious little ones have the eye: little Anna and Eva see the little girl Ève behind the beard. They play together. For my mother it's restful. With big people one has to work at giving the right answers.

22 July 2013

I don't understand. I complain of a morbid incomprehension, a thick cataract that obscures my soul, I let life escape me, escape itself, I was keeping watch I didn't see the step, suddenly, it was the other side, she was up at O.'s place Sunday morning, she comes down in the afternoon and the loss took place in the hallway. Or the abduction. Or the exchange. Something terrible. A bad second. Such a little second. But afterwards one falls for a very long time, the devastating fall goes on for six months. I don't understand, help me, I ask my son for the help of the sciences, turn on the lights! I fall, motionless, endless fall. Does such a mad fall exist? says my terror. It is death, says my son. A brutal fall in slow motion. The gentle and knowledgeable voice of my son calms my chaos. Death! I didn't know. This distraction, this wildness of time, this drop that will fall, the last strand of the rope that has been on the point of rupturing strand by strand for years, the last strand and it is still all of life and already it is death, a minimal oscillation, and one feels each of the thousands of final seconds not pass but explode, break up. It goes so slowly. What pains me is the formation within me of a shadow, that's what death is in me. I understand less and less the imperceptible advance of impotence, the seizing of power by the armies of King Nothingness. Thus, I was undergoing with Maman the experience of the process of mortality, I realise that I was thinking about it abstractly, I believed in the theorem of finitude, outside my body, my heart, like a law of mathematical physics that I would never have known how to apply to my life.

For two years every day I actively took the measurements of the maternal climate. Between 2011 and 2012 the park receded in a spectacular fashion. Saturday, 3 March 2012, I noted a moment that will be entered among the unforgettable ones. In the cold and still wintry park we enter by rue Gazan, because this is where a bench is situated at the least distance from the ice floe. Roro and I are supporting our subject. On the bench, Ève is at the cinema of life. She sees the world in activity, as with a telescope: he's running! she's running! The world is running. She marvels, sitting, childhood, people are running! Me too when I was two years old, a year and a half I used to marvel. To run! That's already the moon. At the corner of the little guard house, a little tree in flower, the only one, no other. Ève is excited. Ève has had enough. –What are we doing here? It's beautiful. That's enough. Ten minutes are perhaps three hours in Ève-duration? My heart hurts. When we used to walk in the park Maman and I, in *the other life, formerly*, three years ago. The progressive shrinking of the park. Terribly palpable, says my son. The park is the instrument for measuring the progressive shrinking. When we did only half the park. When we stopped at the first bench. When we ceased going to the park. When we waited for my son to come by so as to hoist Ève into her car. The sad Benediction of the last stroll: fifty metres with four pauses.

At this moment the park reminds me of the parks and gardens where we used to take long philosophical walks without time limits. I see the day when walking along the bank of the Vincennes lake, I suddenly asked her to reveal the secret of her courage, of her way: of passing through storms without trembling, of having lost father, husband, country, protection, of having had her roots cut, of having been despoiled, of having been imprisoned, of having been robbed, threatened, of not having lost her smile, gaiety, worldwide curiosity, the desire to wander, the pleasure of travelling through the United States in a car with a nonagenarian émigré barely younger and in much worse shape than she, the habit of going out every day to do errands in Paris like the farmer who goes out to his fields every morning, of not having known fear, of having always said yes, of having followed me everywhere except to India, of not having wasted a moment of this long and yet not inexhaustible life, of having the instinct and the honour of conservation, of having collected all the glass jars and recording every evening of her life in the notebooks with moveable pages the *exact* accounts of her expenditures and income for the day. Everything must be taken into consideration, nothing is too insignificant of what goes on in the commerce of life with itself. Any movement is worth any other. She registers the rent from the Strasbourg factory in the credit column. In the debit column, one finds: lift, .80 euro. For future researchers, this sum refers to the lift my mother takes in Arcachon to go from the Winter City to the Summer City, and that brings her to within a hundred metres of the Monoprix. In a thousand years one will be able to reconstitute the existence of a woman who lived in Europe, four hundred years after Shakespeare, more or less at the time of Kafka and the mobile telephone. She wrote on the doors of her home recommendations and addresses for everyday life. Among the books shelved without any apparent order on her book-shelves, the complete Heine in five volumes, *Das Lexikon der Hausfrau, 4500 Stichworte*, Herbst, 1932, Berlin, *Advice and Recipes for Difficult Times*, pub. Gautier-Languerau, 18 rue Jacob Paris 6th, 1941, *Food in Times of Rationing*. Ève perpetually kept survival manuals nearby.

To come back to the bank of the lake, my mother responded to me that the whole secret was contained in the word *life*, it sufficed to enjoy it so long as one had the chance and the possibility. Life does not need justification. It is its own force. My mother is herself the secret. She has it. I don't have it. –And what if you lost me? I say. –That would be terrible, but I would be obliged to go on without you.

The park is done, remain the geraniums. She discovers them every day. It's a new continent. In truth the light assures the sumptuous innovation of the Geranium landscape. Some days one comes upon a shore that seems to be in flames. Sprays of fire of every shade of red explode. She sums up her vigilant presence at my side, in the Green Bean problem: who, when I am no longer there, is going to prepare the greenbeans? In the summer of 2012, I want to record this, the summer of her physical breakdowns, on two occasions I gave her some butter beans to prepare. One lays them on a platter, cuts off their ends with scissors. She got tired. You're not obliged to finish. She was obliged. Beans, the last shield. She didn't read any longer. She cast a quick glance at the geraniums. But she sees the prophetic vegetables through to the end. Almost. Eat them? One or two individuals. We have arrived at the period of purées and soft foods.

9 March 2012. What remains of Maman, beyond, or besides, under-neath the wailings: I decide to go around the children's garden, to extract

her from the sand pit, to dig her up. I show her a letter from Kafka to Milena: '*ich bin nicht unaufrichtig, Milena*'. –What does that mean? I say. –Milena, says Ève, is a name. *Here*, I say, *ici*. I tap beneath the word *unaufrichtig, ici*. Read! Right away she says, very clearly: '*sincere*'. The word *sincere* becomes golden. Thus I've found the vein. Mystery of the synapses. Since, in the jumble of wailings, she can go impeccably from one language to another, here the bridges are not broken down, there, there are no more bridges. Sad happiness: German still lives *aufrichtig*. Thus the languages are not extinguished. They smoulder beneath the ashes of the hundred and two years. They could die buried alive. I stir the ashes.

On 14 March, I go away. I leave her a love letter. 'I will be back at the end of the afternoon,' I write. I don't know how this indication will be treated by her imagination. I will never know. On returning, I find a letter. Ève tried to get hold of a felt-tip pen. Roro handed it to her. She wrote by herself, her letter referring to mine. 'I'm waiting to see you again, my dearest big baby doll. Ève Cixous.' When I enter she cries out: 'I adore you.' Hugs me. Now, my mother never proffers affective utterances. I conclude from this that she must have feared she had lost me. This I-adore-you is the only outpouring of this kind that year. I note it down carefully. Next she prevents me from going onto the balcony, she's afraid. I imagine the visions that make her tremble: the balcony falls. Or the wind carries off her daughter. Hélène no longer returns. I give up the balcony.

Parked. 14 March 2013. I look at us: a desperate jealousy of the us that was and will never be again. Everything that we used to enjoy. This Yesterday banished to the pasts. Our empires, our riches: speaking, desiring, a few steps, even modest ones, rising, admiring the flowers, the luxury of the empire at its end: the wheelchair. The armchair now serves as an antique, an old car no longer in use. Today the world is contained between medicalised bars. I am some twenty centimetres away from my mother. I cannot embrace her. Thus my old dream of incarceration has come true. We are in prison. Together – apart.

20 July 2013

Disproportions, tragic irony: how a short one-minute video (*café liégeois*, do you hear it? I say to my son, I hear *qu'a fait lie et joie*, *café lié joie*, says my son, I hear *qu'as tu fait de ta joie*, what did you do with your joy, I muse), a magical minute, rises up victoriously before the monumental mausoleum of the six months of agony. So there exists a savage struggle between the images of her glory years and those several days when I had the impression that our joyous empire was crumbling into disorder and cowardice. I groped in the shadows, I didn't hear her voice any longer, I who had been fidelity, the ear, the harbour, the cradle. Gothic ideas of murder, the beating of bat wings haunted me, the painful astonishment of having ruined the most beautiful painting with a bad brush stroke.

There had happened what had made of the cruelly theatrical death of my father an indelible catastrophe. I call this misfortune 'the uninterpretable sign'. Standing or sitting behind a raised window the one who is going away makes a sign with his hand. Like this. But I was far away and I was myopic. It was perhaps: like this. Two silent words. What are you saying? screams my heart. Go away? Come back? No? Adieu? The last word is that, it's the one you don't hear, that you don't understand, it's the ring one doesn't catch, it's the stone one strikes two times. And then for weeks I was tortured by the uninterpretable. All signs divide ad infinitum, I don't know what to give, I loved my mother blindly, I say to my son, she said no for yes –do you want to drink? –no, however she drinks, but perhaps this drinking is a non-drinking, and everything is poisoned. And there was no last word, I say, no last word of the last minute, no last minute, it occurs to me that it's I who said the last word, according to her ultimate music, I whispered it into her mouth from which flowed endlessly the recitative in regretful Toolate, *ich bin verloren*, I am lost, *ach! wo ist mein Leben hin, ach! was soll ich der Seele sagen, wenn sie mich ängstlich fragt: Ach wo bin ich hin? wo bist du, Hélène, Hélène?* Pain awakens me. Then at midnight I question the white Matisse notebook, and my notebook reassures me: she said the last word that Sunday, and it was my name. She was pitying us with my name.

That photo has the power to give her back to me in reality, suddenly there she is on the balcony very much alive and as accessible as the balcony on which I am writing this July when there is no one in her room and yet her whole person is there. I put her white cap on her. She is sitting in the armchair, it's hot, she is absorbed in reading *Cousin Pons*, I am not re-seeing her, I see her. Nothing has changed. She has not lost the power of speech: the scene is naturally silent. I don't disturb her. I look at her and smile. I take note of her. In this instant, we are. Ève is reading.

While I am writing, she is reading, below on the balcony. While I am writing she waits for me.

She was changing. Say I to my son 15 July 2013. Two weeks after the Change. This happened in fits and starts. In leaps. I didn't see it. I had a suspicion. I would ask: do you find her changed? Everyone answered: no. That would surprise me. I was late, or she was ahead of me, or the other way around, I was going first, she stopped, slipped, started again. I was doubting. At least at night nothing happens: I find her again in the position where I had seen her fall asleep the night before her head bent at an angle, her nose at the exact point where I had left it. There had been no time. Time starts up again. Nothing changes, I would say to myself. After the crash of 13 January, the brutal cave-in, the cries, the bloody accident, the collapse into the procession of the Medicalisedbed, the rout, things are stable. Do you see anything? I would ask myself. What there is to see is invisible at that moment. There is imminence in the air. Imminence is undetectable. Odourless. Suddenly one wants to weep. Sometimes nothing. It's in the thoughts, a bristling, a pang, an unbelievable fatigue. There is some attack and one takes flight. The habitual stubbornness gives up the fight. One begins to write a page and a great lassitude spreads, one lets it drop. It's like the treacherous voice of the antidream demon, the internal heckler who preaches betrayal of myself: betray yourself, don't exert yourself, lie down and sleep. *Sleep* falls. *Glas.* Save your breath! Rhymes with death, says my mother.

I was late and delayed realising it, I sinned out of laziness, lack of experience of laziness, and the impossibility of finding the strength to work.

Here I will cite the day of the Great Fault: how I got angry with Ève on 3 September 2012. Not all at once but progressively. A 4 o'clock *p.m.* she had the impression of being saved, of finding Maman (me) again, the way one sets foot again on land. Like the time I had the impression of being pulled out of hell when, at three years old, I found my mother again. At the instant of salvation, she emits her cry: 'Help me! Help me! What are you doing for me. Where are you?' A chasm-demand. A gaping cry. Out of the abyss she calls endlessly. A need to call in order to fill up the chasm. Nothing interests her any more in the world except the hole, the abyss, the call, the cry. No one exists except the *idea*-of-Maman. I am there, but I am not there. She calls Maman. I try to make myself into Maman, to make myself into bread, milk. At the table I serve her spinach purée. *È.* –Not good. It's black. *H.* –It's green, eat it, it's good. It's your recipe. *È.* –No. So some soft egg yolks. She looks at the devilled eggs with anger: Not for me! Not good! I take away the eggs. The two round golden cakes, driven out. Not good! Don't want it. Then my voice, calmly, deposits six words in front of her, a plate with six black and golden words: You're a pain in the arse. Then I observe the sentence. No smoke rises. It is not black. My mother also looks at it. Doesn't give a damn. Nothing like the explosion of 'You are two imbeciles' of Jean Santeuil.

–Don'tgiveadamn, says my-mother-the-child.

The mother-me wonders: did the stubborn one hear? See the six spinach words? Doesn't give a damn.

I repeat clearly: –Don'tgiveadamn? You're a pain in the arse.

She says, with a vaguely surprised or interested air: *Weshalb?* Why do you say that?

I say: –Because you said no seven times.

She says: –I did that? No!

Me: –Do you want to go to bed?

She, brightly: –Yes! Help me. Helpmeeehelpmee.

We leave the room. The chair rolls toward the bedroom. –Where are we going? –To bed. –Helpmeee. Where are we going? Where are you? All her sentences begin with the tonic accent on the first syllable. Scansion in the hallway: –Hé-lène! Where are you? Wherewegoing? –To bed. –Where's that? –At the bottom of the world, one descends, it's long, it's slow, one moves in a spiral eight metres unfold over heavy and identical weeks, black syrup of time, a mad progression into the worst, perpetual, ungraspable, there is no moment, there is no choice, there is no question, Maman's questions are not posed, they flutter their deranged parrot wings stuffed with straw, much later we are in the bedroom. On the verge of going to bed fully dressed, the parrot lying on her back suddenly weighs a hundred kilos. –Wait! I cry. We take off the slacks. –*Weshalb?* –Wait! We take out the teeth. –My teeth! Where are my teeth? Poor little teeth! They are already sleeping. I'm afraid! They are going to get lost. –They're waiting for you. They'll be there tomorrow. –That's far. –*Goodnight. Goodnight sweet prince*

At that moment, in the bedroom, such a great sorrow took hold of me that I still feel it today gnawing my heart without anaesthesia. I am still eleven months later in the scalded state caused by a me come out of my wild obscurities and there is no one to plead an explanation, what is done is done, at that moment, once Maman was in bed and peacefully sleeping, the suffering assailed me, I began to throw myself in sobs on Maman's little body, as if I could wash away with my tears the blasphemy that I had cast upon her, it was a desperate trick of my imagination, in reality I was incurable and I knew it, I was suffering as if I had abjured Maman me who adores her (I write this on 23/7/13 having put on my mother's little beige vest that I believe or imagine is still impregnated with her odour) as violently as if I had had a hand cut off, a hand torn out of my soul, I heard myself screaming inside. I was mortally put out with this me who had got angry with Maman and it was me.

It was the fault of French. I would have liked to say that phrase in German. –How does one say 'pain in the arse' in German. –Don't know. –Try. –Doesn't exist in German. The weight, the matter of insults, varies according to language. In my language, this uncommon expression has the volume and the gravity of words punished by a Dantesque frost.

Is it the beige vest or the writing? I suffer less from this icy burning. Not that there is a remedy. But at least there is here proof of a certain courage that the cowardly soul latches on to. One knows that nothing, neither time nor confession, will ever erase this stain. One toppled over, from one second to the next, into the incurable. When one writes *Lord Jim* or *Macbeth*, it is not in the hope of inventing multitudinous seas to wash away the tarnish. It is to erect a monument to the fault, so as not to flee it in the next sin, the second cowardly act. Only 'Maman' will extinguish the biting mark when I rejoin her, if I rejoin her on the other side, if there is another side. Think of Rousseau. I hasten to rejoin Maman. This haste is a mad thing, an impatience that cannot take its own measure. Since 1 July it has taken up a place in my heart, in the form of the sensation of a perpetual race. I have changed leitmotif. Before I used to say to Ève: I am here. Now I say: I am coming.

But however inexorably present it is, this scene could have taken place only in those faraway years when Ève was still speaking, when I would dress her and undress her, when we would confront together the different ordeals that each day was preparing for us, the difficult meals, the ruined beaten broken exhausted evenings, the small victories in the toilet. The word toí-let! sounding the alert as if from the height of a foreyard, the frenetic state of the crew, the goings-to-bed that resembled rescues, and one reached the grace of the bed with the relief of the shipwrecked.

But in 2013 I no longer dress her, I merely change her nightgown in January, and in February we reach the stage of putting on only the pyjama top so as to avoid all painful contact with the part of her body, her upper thighs, that was not bandaged and where morning and evening I seek a spot to plant the little syringe among the innumerable seedlings of the haematomas.

It's Ève's Change that I cannot manage to think, I say to my son. Change, says my son, is where Greek mathematics stops: the impossibility for the Greeks to think change. I am arrested by the Change. I had merely to look at her for a long time and I found her again in 2013, it was Ève, there was no longer any change. We were living in a perfectly ordered way. Her body was losing strength, mobility, but I didn't know when. Not from one day to the next. No more than me. What is more some of the changes that I thought I had noticed were cancelled all at once. We retraced our steps, in reverse, back to the beginning. She no longer spoke. Suddenly long after the silence the mutism gave way. She was speaking. A whole day come from another year.

When did It begin? The progression, I mean. We were in progress, tottering. In September 2012 she expresses herself with monosyllables or interjections. The Dictionary of Ève's cries on this date: *Warum? Weshalb? Tut weh!* No more! That's enough! No! Don'tgiveadamn!

She lets out a loud piercing cry when the toilet flushes. As if she were the excrement. *Ah!*

In the bedroom, saved. She goes to bed dressed. –Wait, I say. You have to undress. –Why? –You're a pain in the arse, I say to this intruder me. Why so many obstacles? We could both go to bed, without undressing, protect each other, without disarming. *Sich umarmen. Arm* the beautiful word 'arm' in German makes me weep. *Arm. Arme* Ève. *Arme Hélène.* Poor, poor!

I run from January to July 2013, I run a race made up of an infinity of stages that are longer and longer shorter and shorter. Since 10 July I have been writing so as not to interrupt the race that brings Ève back to me.

Blind, I say to my son, overtaken by Ève's speed, she had left me in the dust, I was behind, I didn't see her take the step. Didn't want to see that she no longer wanted to eat. I judge myself: guilty. Ève's state in September 2012: Don'tgiveadamn. Clear message. The new bathroom, conceived for a small invalid: Don'tgiveadamn. Her haunting question: Why, why? She tries in German: *Warum? Weshalb?*

Weshalb appears in September, coming from very far away. The double and half of *Warum.* I look it up in the etymological dictionary. Not at *Wes.* I find it at *Halb.* An extraordinary word. I receive it like a jewel that Maman gives me quickly. She has no fancy jewellery. *Halb,* half, is the second member, the other hand of one hand the other. Maman is, halfway, elsewhere, *autre part. The Other Part(s).* The other departs, she remains. Or else: she is the one who departs, the other. The other always departs. She departs, she cries out in terror. Cries of the summer. Since we are undivided, when she cries I shudder with terror.

Why did I not analyse her cries of terror during the month of August 2012? Respond! Having reached the limit of my force of resistance, the 'big boss' gives up. Fatigue. A siege of three years, which does not say its name. All the stupidities done by the Trojans and the Greeks after a certain time. Desertion. Narcissistic withdrawal. On both sides they exhale. Enough! They break camp. After so many years. They stop the damage. Life stops, death stops. The two sides have been frozen for five years, dead sails, cancelled voyages, the world shrivelled into a tiny portion of Asia Minor. I restrict myself to the immediate. Then I *receive the cry* in the face, in the belly. I no longer read. –I no longer read Maman. I didn't accompany her. Since when? Precisely I can't answer. Since Too Much. The Too Much is there quickly. Avoid avoiding the truth. I became limited. I took my stand. What does Montaigne say about my case? I am sure that he speaks of this indolence through the drying up of concern, of that programmed failing of the human machine.

Urgency: make up for the delay at least this one, return to her, that is, to Maman-me, make *half* with *halb*. *Halbieren, mediare,* bring to an end. On the 3rd in the evening I change the diet. We don't eat black or yellow things any more. We nibble. Everything is going fine. We are camped now on a steppe. The light is beautiful. Sunday, 10 September 2012, in the room where she's in bed, from afar she makes a mischievous little sign with her index finger. –Shhh! Who are you? –I'm the wolf, I say, and I'm going to eat you. –The wolf? –You hear me? I cry. –Yes! I am nude! I am nude and crude.

And impishly she goes back to sleep.

On 29 September getting up, a large puddle of pee. Ève impishly points to it: 'It's the bird. Did you see?'

È. –One hundred and two years old. That's not good. *Marthe the physio.* –How old are you? *È.* –Wahwah. *Marthe the physio.* –It's your birthday Madame Cixous. How old? *È.* –Forty. Hélène, how old will I be? I am very old. *H.* –Do you want to know your true age? *È.* –Yes. *H.* –One hundred and two. *È.* –That's a lot. That's not good. Thirsty! Thirsty!

That evening, she lets out a loud cry: –Ah!!! *Roro.* –Why are you crying? *È.* –Because I am mad. One hundred and two years old is too much. Itscaresme. *H.* –You can be less. No one will know. *È.* –That's good. *The neighbour.* –How old are you? *È.* –Eighty. *The neighbour.* –Ah! I'm older than you. I'm eighty-four. *È.* –That's a lot. Poor old guy.

Between 14 January 2013 and the 22nd, we oscillate. She gets weaker. She holds on. I fear, I don't fear, I fear. What? I don't stop fearing until fear exhausts itself, then fear takes off again. My fear and Ève's state precipitate each other, take diverging paths, disagree, refute each other, like two opposite storms.

I believe one must defend Literature, the land of turbulences and of the perpetual disqualification of states of mind.

Tuesday, 22 January, she comes out of death like out of the shower, in fine form, I sit her before the window, *and she sees*. 'A lot of snow! A lot of cars. Ohlala!' Long sentences, strong affects. –There is light! There are cars! Oh! Now there are no more! There're no cars? Hélène, where are the cars! What is that over there, the light?

–Life! Life! I say.

Wednesday the 23rd the grey sky darkens. There are no more cars. The first word is *kaput*. Ève rigid, black with wounds. Repeats: drink! no! drink! no! Enough. No! Drink! Wants doesn't want no to drink no doesn't want wants, to live, wants. Wants.

At noon, she has an adventure: everyone has disappeared. 'I was worried,' she says. 'I said: there is no one any longer. As for me I was alone. I said: where did they go? I got worried. Where were you? Here? There's a restaurant here? You had lunch? What did you eat? There's a dining room? Oh okay! And me, I didn't eat? I said: everyone has disappeared. Some tea? That's not nourishing. As for me I was alone.'

That day my mother talks for a long time, she goes to the restaurant of words, she shows her appetite. She wants to sit down at the table with the living. Tell them her bad dream.

This will be the last adventure. Afterwards there will be no more stories, never.

'*Leave-me!*' says Ève. These are the first words in her English period that begins on 28 January. Leave me! The strange assails her. She retaliates. Perhaps the enemy understands English.

Medicalisedbed, that's the first word of this other language, which I am going to learn to speak, a zoo of signifiers with Greek roots for the most part.

On 30 January the Screaming hurricane is unleashed. I have never lived through such a tempest. One believes that the gusts of cries are going to crash down in an hour-long storm. That's a mistake. Secret, unknown forces exist that exceed our calculations and our human possibilities. The assault is sustained at a supernatural degree of intensity for several hours. As if life were heaved up by an inextinguishable anger, and was very intent on making it felt. Ève proffers tirelessly. Her soul the eagle flies over the body that, from the blows of fate, has succumbed, while shouting out great cries.

È. –I believed everything

I lost everything
I believed I believed
I am lost
I hurt everywhere
Not the pain that hurts me
Hélène! Help me! Help me, my little mama
I believed in you
Toolate, it's toolate, everything's finished
Ich bin verloren
Hélène, Doll, my little doll, where are you?
What are you thinking?
H. –And you?
È. –*Café au lait*, that's all.
I want something else.
H. –What?
È. –*Café au lait* that's all.
Enough too much. I want something else
Enough! Drink! Drunk enough!
I want to drink. Where is the water.
That's enough. Not drink! A little water that's all
That's enough for me and that's all
Me, I'm thinking of something else
What is happening to me?
It costs how much?
Help me, I am lost.
Toolate. What do you want me to do?
H. –What do you want me to do?
È. –I believed I believed
I want I want.
H. –What do you want? Tell me what you want. I will do it. (Do you
want the endless sleep?)
È. –*Café au lait*.
I want to sleep. Leave me alone
Enough! Enough! DRUNK enough
I want to boire! *I want to bed*
I want to go to bed

During the recitative, I take notes, sad so sad to be able to capture
only the rhythm of the suffering and not at all the substance of the voice
that is so strong, so weak, so amazingly melodic despite the crack in the
timbre that I had the impression of hearing sung the very moving chorale
of Bach's Old Age

Wenn ich einmal soll scheiden
So scheide nicht von mir
Wenn ich den Tod soll leiden
So tritt du dann herfür

I wept floods onto my paper. I gave her to drink *café-au-lait*-that's-all, a drink that I suspected was not what she expected, that she rejected exclaiming: 'It'snotgood! it's not *café-au-lait*-that's-all. Enough! Hélène! I want another pill.' I have to think something.

On 2 February enters the Medicalisedbed. It materialises so brutally that I lose its hidden meaning. Deliberately hideous, as is only right for a beast from Herebelow, head and feet in fake mahogany, rancid, dirty, without neutrality, the look of a verdict. That it wounds me is another feature of my denial of reality. My mother is now behind bars. Until this day in February I was able to lie down by her side as I did when I was eleven years old and had become my father and her defender. The vehicle might have been a work of art, but it's a work of severity: bow down! A decision rises within me, hesitates, murmurs: and what if the two of us ran way to the garden in Arcachon? –Don't be ridiculous, creaks the bed. My vague impulse fades.

Ève's text, in English: *To bed! To bed! I want to bed!*

I obey. Distant echoes of Macbeth.

I no longer know who among me brought the Medicalised bed into our flanks, it's as if I had given into the charms of the Trojan horse, I said to myself, I lived it like a defeat, like a confession of my limits. The benefits, I distrusted them, to be sure she will no longer fall out of bed, I will no longer find her, tangled up, her legs folded around the legs of the toilet-chair. The tribe of fear that she might fall is dispersed. I will stop getting up three times a night, being haunted by false phantoms.

End of surprises. End of shipwrecked nights. An unsinkable boat.

Medicalisedbed coincides with her internal immobility: she no longer moves. As if she had swallowed the unshakable structure of the metal.

Unforgettable final scene: installation of the prison vessel. Quick. Quicker. During its assembly, Ève broken, Ève dislocated in her last armchair, in pain, cannot sit up. To bed! To bed! Poor captain who wants to perish as quickly as possible. And then the mattress with pulses of air, an artificial wave, whose intermittent humming becomes the strange music of the voyage.

I could go out. No more risks of escape. I don't go out. Something prevents me from leaving the dock. As if now spiritual downfalls might happen. She might fall internally. The iron armature makes her fragile. I never left her alone. At least I believe that. Who knows what makes up solitude?

There is something indefinable in the bed that belongs to another world. I could not put myself in Maman's place in that – thing – that vehicle of arrest.

Instructions for use: one opens the cage by lowering the bars in order to give care or meals. One closes it again.

The Anger of the Scamander

In February 2013 I begin rereading the Iliad. *I'm looking to encounter Ajax, the one who loses his immense glory a certain evening. The* Iliad *was waiting for me. Its atrocious delights. Everyone is going to die. Everyone is expecting to die. One cannot live without dying. One avoids dying only by suspending life beneath one's tent. I can no longer stop reading the* Iliad: *it's the same scenario chant after chant, they fight, they kill, they die, they are going to die they present themselves at the contest, they state their names, genealogies, what beautiful characters they will have been, they kill each other in song, I wish that it would never end, the song, the blood, the flood of bodies, the anger of the Scamander who has had E-nough E-nough of being full of cadavers I feel it personally, what is this story of overdying, this agony whose end is known and whose length in time and space is unknown.*

My mother has been ready for the last act since the year 2000 and all armour-plated with bandages for a year, no one is ignorant of who is going to win what who is going to lose what, who, living now extends beyond

And during this time Mandela lying like Maman in a Medicalisedbed wanders motionless the borderless shores

Categories of modern suffering take shape, rise up before our thoughts, in a haze their anxious silhouettes are the Nearby Shades, those representing Maman and Mandela as alreadydead stilliving. The majority of the populations parade before the layer of pioneers in a state of respectful uneasiness. One doesn't know what they are thinking. One cannot interrogate them. They are themselves every day in a new state whose laws they do not know. Researchers specialised in the study of these exceptional longevities are in training, they have no model, they advance by hypotheses and errors into these zones that are only begin-ning to reveal their outlines. The scouts are themselves mistaken about their own fate. Nobody knows anything. The question of 'knowledge' is a major problem. Everyone senses that it is a veritable pharmakon: *a psychic substance that is both desirable and dreadful which at any moment can prove to be poison itself. One senses, without proof, that the simple fact of knowing what one does not not know but that one keeps under a veil can precipitate a 'fatal outcome'. Well, one doesn't know, if one has not lived it, and there is the aporia that opens its python jaws in front of us, whether one desires or repels this precipitation. One cannot know it: the pioneers advance while oscillating from one shore to the other.*

My mother conducted her funeral in the smallest details and in her language, in the year 2005. She chose the wood of her casket, without hesitation. That's good. We follow her to the letter. What delivers the execution of her recommendations over to a poetic indecision is a detail that constitutes her matchless signature: it's a matter of the hereafter famous article, called 'minimumrabbi'. This minimumrabbi delights me. No one will ever be able to interpret with certainty the neological expression of my mother's will. She herself would doubtless have had no precise idea of what the minimumrabbi might be once the day arrived. This opening to surprise is an enchanted door on the future. Another kind of surprise is the caution she firmly maintained concerning the property aspect of the home that does not interest her herself. She never wanted to precede herself. Not to go alive to the cemetery has remained her tradition. When, in 2008, we had to decide on a precise address, my daughter and I, we were given a quarter of an hour to respond, I saw nothing but a sea of petrified waves, I hung onto my daughter's arm, I had just time to phone Ève so as to describe the neighbourhood for her briefly. She asks me: 'is it accessible?' I say: 'there are three steps, not very high'. So she agrees. She has always watched out for the accessible. It's the first and decisive degree of her philosophy. When they go into battle, while their companions are dressing them in their heavy armour, our heroes know and don't know. The important thing is to go into battle. One can go there only under the aegis of ambivalence. When the day arrived for her grandmother, Helene Jonas, in 1924 in Osnabrück, the whole family gathered around her and Doctor Pelz said: 'Are you content, Frau Jonas? Your children are all here. Not one is missing.' So Helene Jonas thought it's terrible. They are all standing and dressed except for me. Me I'm nude and crude. And she said: 'It's good and it's not good.' Until 2013 I believed that the story Ève told me was truthful. Suddenly I learned, I think it was in May, that it was a fable, a true fable. I was looking at my mother in her boat. She no longer spoke. She no longer opened her eyes. A hundred people would not have made a mother, on the contrary, one wants Maman at that moment, and for her to say to us: I am here, I stay with you, my love, as always. No. Don't say. Stay.

What is an illusion?

I am asking myself this on 4 February 2013, Monday's dawn is black. Since Sunday, 13 January, it's war. Massive invasion. The night is motionless. I do the rounds. At 4 o'clock in the morning. At 5 o'clock. At 6.30. She is sleeping. She is sleeping? Then the chant rises strongly: helpmee, helpmee. Ate: six soupspoonfuls of compote. The body is deserted. The giant force is in her hands, to push away.

–I hurt. –Where? She points to the corner of her mouth. I laugh. –What is wrong with my foot? –Your foot is black. I laugh for her. Who could have imagined that so much blood would come to make her something like a supplementary foot, black in colour? She is sleeping. Sitting around the bed, the Feelings. Diffuse, timid, uncertain. A slight nearfar phantom, passes, I prick up my ears, what if she departed in her sleep? The unforeseeable commands *everything*. I will spend the coming months surrounded by a troop of phantoms, illusions, and a choir of Greek and German premonitions, a restless mixture of hope-anxiety, of sticky hope that is contested, scanned, tick-tock, beddy-bye, I sleepwatch, life passes, purrs, I caress her in my thoughts, she comes and puts her cat's bottom on my notebook, in the street the noise of the rubbish collectors, I pick up the debris in my notebooks; Ève's bedroom awakens to a pharmaceutical frenzy; little by little great quantities of bandages reside on the shelves. –I'm afraid, says Ève. –Of what? –Afraid of *all that*. –Oh! me too, I think, I'm afraid of *allthat*. Fear is just that, a fear as big as Ève, faceless, that enters into the house of the body while roaring like the lorry of the rubbish collectors, and that stays sitting on its bottom like a stupefied sphinx. One doesn't dare. One doesn't finish. Little by little the footless sentences, the headless thoughts multiply, one walks without legs, I write without words, holes replace the roads. One sees only by turning around. One advances backwards. Then one day I take note: today it has been three months since she has said: that's good. I am unaware of that but my white notebook tells me. Three blank months, let it pass, notforme. They have not passed, not in front of me.

–You will help me? says Ève. I pass the fear with her.

'She is fading,' says O., 'what do you imagine, slowly.'

I imagine the slowness of slowly, I contemplate the equal splendour of the candle, what is slowness, everything is division, I note in fact a slowing down of my pace of life I eat little, I sleep hardly at all, a curfew extends to the whole City, the events, seen from the bed, are so small that they are interchangeable, all the heads of government in the world are the same nasty little man, ambitious and cowardly, who was called Agamemnon.

'What do you imagine? That she is going to get back up?'

Ah! There it got me: it's the words *get back up* that strike me, I don't know why.

I listen. Not the words. The whisperings of the heart. Do I believe? I don't believe. What strength it requires to stand up without the rigid energy of believing, out of pure necessity, that is to say, out of love, out of love for poor love, the love that says yes, humbly, sans power, sans army, sans *everything*, and that can only shore up its infinite weakness on the tenacity of illusions.

–You have illusions, says O.

Now that is indeed something I have. Later I will note down my illusions of 4 February 2013. That evening, Victoire says: she's the one who is driving. She repeats the sentence to me nine times. Driving. As if she were coating me with a salve. Driving. That's Ève to a T. She always drove. For her burial, everything's done, since 2008. Driving. Have to follow her, says Victoire. –Where we going? says Ève. I look up at Victoire. –Follow her. I have the feeling that Victoire is trying to send me a message and that she has the feeling that I resist and that I resist this feeling, that I'm turning around myself, around where, Ève says: –Where we going? –Into the bedroom. *Ève*. –Where is the bedroom? I say: –Here? Ève. –There. We go. Slowly, from feeling to feeling, by the light of sentences whose batteries are low we drag ourselves in a labyrinth of remurmurs and resistances. What is she saying to me, I say to myself, wanting to say to me, me wanting to say? I end up saying to myself that I've received messages that I don't know how to translate. Bad at translation. All these messages respond with interrogation. I make a little train with Ève's song: Wherearewegoing wegowhere wegowherewego. Or else I translate 'docilely': 'She is fading.' But right away the sentence fades beneath a flood of images.

Maman comes home from the market like a victorious general. We take the booty out of the boot of the Reno. She is radiant beneath her white hat. On the kitchen table, the beans for the sacrifice (they replace the lamb that replaces Isaac). The eggplants are planted there. The radishes are ravishing. Everything rhymes. There is a very ugly cotton nightgown made in China for five euros we can throw it away I will never be able to throw it away. History wants it that my mother and the Chinese seamstress be cut from the same cloth without knowing it. The priceless price of the inexpensive object. I imagine my mother attending Mme Li in childbirth and they agree to a price.

But that was in the year 2000. The vision fades like a burnt-out candle. 'She is fading, says O.' There perhaps still remains the seller of cotton nightgowns at the market. For a few seconds Maman still glows then she is lying down. Even the idea that she will never again go to the market doesn't move.

I should sleep with her. At 5 o'clock in the morning I come in. Ève's eyes flutter quickly: –Pee! Gay. *H*. –Sleep! Go in your pants. It is too early, that is to say tooearlylate, too early in too late. Alone, I cannot lift Maman. We wait for Roro, I say. –Roro!, say the skipping eyes. Too bad that I cannot lift her and put her on the pot. With eyes so light, the bird weighs a ton, the toneless body, the rigid legs, the shining eyes. Fade? There is nothing more lively than that fire, I say to myself. Stronger than the ashes.

I don't understand why the legs don't follow. I don't understand.

–I believed she was going to survive the old life and resuscitate.

–But you believed she was going to die?

–I believed it one evening and in the morning I believed from the other side.

I do not buy nightgowns at the market, I don't have my mother's naïve faith. I'm happy she had the faith I don't have. Without her I would not have lived at least one totally modest life. Go to the market!, I say to the shade of my mother. My voice has the same power to incite as the one I exercise over the cats: go, Philia! And the cat goes. And my mother goes to market. The shade of Ève answers me, at least for the moment.

–Where are we going? Victoire says: –She's the one who is driving. Ève is sleeping peacefully. She invents dream driving, without chauffeur, without *goal*, astral, leaning on me. –Where wegoing? We are escaping.

Everything that Ève gives me: her extreme politeness, her responsibility, her naturalness. One is a body that has seen others. Two hundred and forty childbirths a month. She always says thank you, goodbye, *goodnight*. To Roro: –Thank you! *Roro:* –Thank you who? *Ève well-behaved:* –Thank you, Roro. To Fatima: Thank you … I-sabelle. *Fatima.* –Oh! Isabelle? No. Fa-?

–Fa-? Ève thinks then triumphs: Fanny!

To H., in English: –Hélène, *I want to sleep. H*. –Until when? *È*. –Until this evening, where wegoing.

Unrepresentable: Ève, a month ago, standing, lifts one foot, obeys the physio, asks for her armchair. To sit down. Never again. The bedsores look at me, with a viscous eye. Painless? The assault began a month ago, says my diary. A month but unleashed, screaming, interminable. The citadel holds out. She might discourage death, why not? In my opinion, she is playing a trick on the assailant. H. a little shaken by others' convictions. 'Alittle', as Ève says. Half-Ève. The legs don't respond any longer. The arms hold the steering wheel. Alittle is fading.

But there is a morning in February while wheelchairing her where she is wedged among six cushions, her head leaning on her right shoulder, she says a sentence: 'You saw the sun?' And it's a sentence from the time when she was making sentences.

9 February, the day she saw the sun.

Next comes the stolen sentence on the nurse's voice mail, the loud-speaker turned on, by chance or not. A voice says: 'Mme Cixous has the air of someone who doesn't realise the state of her mother.' I put aside the tone of this voice that doesn't know it was heard by the said Mme Cixous.

Until April 2012, she was making sentences that looked like her, free, ordered, exclamatory sentences in which, to season them, she slipped in the spice of an idiomatic French expression, dare-dare, au diable vauvert.

In the country from which no traveller returns Ève speaks English. It might have been German, her maternal and sororal language. But Ève was always a born traveller. English, language of departure, Osnabrück–London. The language conquered by the young Ève. Her language abroad. When one doesn't know where one has washed up, one is not going to ask directions in Spanish.

I want to sleep, in English. Roro has trouble. She wants a *slip*? Roro guesses. *I want to eat*.

Sometimes the interpretation is made difficult. *I want to* boire. Enough-a-little! To drink all drunk. Hasdrunk to drink. Spectres of drunkenness. Thus she invents, tinkers, transmits the unstable language of the country of dangers and difficulties. It happens that English is sometimes laced with a bit of German. These are SOS's, cries of despair, there is nothing more to expect.

Time: heavy, quasi-coagulated. The length of this month (February 2013): a year. Last time I saw my two children, my wings, my aids: last year, in January. February is a heavy year.

I see coming my father's 12 February, removed from the world of the living behind the last windowpane. Would Ève celebrate it sixty-five years later? H. is doubtful. In times of distress as in times of peace, Ève has never remembered Georges. Her love is H. –And what if all the same? –If what? –One can live from this life that sleeps. Another invention of Ève's. A sleeping life. I could work. H. is already tamed by Medicalisedbed: because of its mobility. On one side it prevents Ève from giving us the slip, on the other it raises, lowers, produces semblances of movement. Makes like a camel. Ève made the mistake of getting on the camel in a skirt and with her handbag. This time she is wearing only a T-shirt. Around her, it's the desert.

She Comes Back to Arcachon

27 July 2013. I spend this month whose door she opened – and together we passed through a cement tunnel on the other side of time – in our house as in this Mutterleib, this motherbody in which one night we dreamed of spending a life. Mutterleib is a sweet armoire of secrets: it holds surprises in store for me. Maman left there an unknown number of messages. The general message is: I am still here. She returns, sometimes from totally unexpected hiding places. One sees fate lending a hand. Here's one: the flood of the 26th, the first of our history, at first I wept about it, saying: Ève never saw such a catastrophe. Then I laughed: the water chased out from beneath Mutterleib's knees four fat cardboard trunks that Ève had forgotten there in 1962, so say the newspapers that look as if they've been buried alive when we find them upon opening. And each of these four fossils bears a title written in white chalk by my mother. They summarise: we left Osnabrück in 1934, we were in London, we were in Paris in 1935, we were in Oran in 1936, in 1947 in Algiers, next we were sent to France to Sainte-Foy-la-Grande in 1959, from there we went back to Algiers and we came back in 1962 to Arcachon, all alone, by way of maritime shipping services. And until this flood, we held up very well. And now, we are dead. We've given up the cardboard ghost.

'Eurydice?' says an A4 sheet that my hand pulls from a bundle of paper beneath my table.

–You know Eurydice? I read. And right away I recognise, I hear Ève answer, ici, ici, ici: *–I don't remember anything. She was unhappy, I think. It's not from my time, it's very old. Who is it?*

Then I answered her: she's the wife of Orpheus.

And now I say to Ève, precipitously so as to hold onto her with my words, here, today, sitting in the little desk chair – while looking at her in the large eyes of her shadow: Eurydice! my darling, it's you! Do not fade! Stay! and as long as I hold this paper beneath my pen, fate acts, pins her down beneath my supplication, I sense she is going to dash off, wait! I'm not Orpheus, it's Hélène, do you hear me? She nods her head. Twice. She does what she can.

White sheets: *we know that the night of 26 to 27 of July 2013 the region was struck by the cyclone Urlage, it's the first time.*

The house was flooded. Ève will thus not have lived through this phenomenon. I regret that. I am delighted by that. I already hear her cries of terror, if she had been hit by the extreme violence of the gusts.

The whole ground floor is under water. It is only two days later that we thought to bring out from deep within the cupboard under the stairs the suitcases that have been sleeping there for fifty years without ever being disturbed. Four wide and tall Koffer

And on one large trunk, the words: White sheets, traced in large chalk letters by my mother's hand.

How not to see in this event a kind of allegorical postcard from the gods?

All these great white linens asleep for centuries brought back beneath the gaze of the survivors

On 9 February 2013. 'You saw the sun.'

I say: –When? Victoire says: –Ève wants to sleep. She has lost two and a half litres of blood. –Mme C. has the air of not realising, says the voice from another world. She will not come back to Ève. –Ève? There are so many of them in her backpack. When? I say. Me, I am with Maman, I say. I'm the one who packs her suitcase. Victoire says: –A doctor cannot predict exactly. But I, your angel appointed to flutter above Eurydice for the suitcase, four weeks, six, at most eight. Right before 'eight', what was I thinking? I have already forgotten. I was thinking: at least the year, I think. Eight, I want to go to sleep. I remain unshaken. Thoughts: eight (not four) to live together, a love story, I know, I have already loved already died, lived eight. Do not lose a minute of them. Do not let yourself be distracted or separated, I run, one must run calmly at top speed, *take* time. Between us (Mamanme), never any secret. –Never?

I believe Victoire. At 5 o'clock in the afternoon, I believe. Around 5.30 an Incredulity takes shape. I believe and don't believe. Little by little I take Maman's side. –Wherewegoing? –We continue. Nothing dead or dying in her. Totally divided, as if I was reading the future in a newspaper, which I don't credit at all. We are several. I never know what I know. I the other. I carry on various activities and thinkings, we cross paths, the contradictions stand like brooms in a corner, they don't bother anyone.

Victoire was afraid of a hip fracture. Me too. Now: very calm departure, without pain thinks Victoire.

Without-pain I thought is not without pain. Don't think about it, I thought.

Don't tell anyone, I say to myself.

My need: to keep the secret so as *to live in the present* with Ève. Don't risk any shock with the feelings of others. Keep death alive between us, ultimate life, benediction. Problem: tell my son or not? Do not deprive my son. I will tell him. After. I climb on board with Ève. Joy with Ève. Programme: joy, virgin joy. The day Ève saw the sun.

Dawn, 10 February, snow, Ève's regular breathing in the dark. Peace. For two weeks when going to Ève in the early morning I was asking myself what the short hours of the night held in store for me. Each time, Ève at her post, quiet.

Immense benediction: she does not hurt, does not complain. A dream voyage. The only down side: the violence of the chamber pot. It's like an attack. She screams. But there is the other attack: the ill-being in pee, *caca*. If only one could economise matter. I can't find a good response. The body is working. The mystery grows, weighs on me; everything's fine, and yet she is departing? 'It's okay,' she says, brief. Watching over the expenditure of energy. Eight weeks? That's far, as Ève would say. They will last perhaps eight months. Who will ever be able to measure the duration of these months? They are perhaps longer or deeper or higher than many years that are as if one had left them on a foreign shelf without reading them.

Times have not yet changed at all. The reign of Ève. Triumph of the Present.

A Sunday like another, she wants: to sleep. No *pipi*. *Sleep*. I embrace her belly. She says: '*goodnight*'. Translation: go away, let me sleep. She remains immersed twenty-four hours. We bring her out of the arms of the refuge, by force. I say: 'good night'. I say to my daughter: I don't *believe*. Knowing is not believing. Like with the little one. In 2005, I don't believe what I know. Life has the strength of faith. There is no future. I see the sun: Ève is just like herself. Weak, exhausted. But what does that mean? Ariane on the phone: 'I'm at the theatre. A beautiful play, interesting for us.' I extend to her my-voice-for-Ariane, fresh, firm, welcoming. Ève's cradle behind my back, invisible. Life: more than one theatre.

13 February 2013. My father died yesterday. It's the sixty-fifth per-formance. Each time that I see the play, I feel the same shock, alone, the death of my father, alone, everything is cut off, decapitation of the heart.

My 2013 solitude at the heart of which I am with her, not alone, my old baby my love.

I must describe her last body, the one that came in January 2013. I can't manage it. It fights back. It flees. It hides. It gets replaced by one of her vigorous, obstinate bodies, even the one she still had when she was a hundred years old and that was much stronger than mine.

The head is intact. The body is eaten away. The others don't see it. She pulls the sheet up to her chin. She defends her house. On her back, facing the enemy, she supports herself, her right hand holds her head that her neck doesn't carry. Later her two hands hold each other on her chest.

She loses control of her mouth in June. It's through there that she is attacked, struck, pierced, poured. Everything is closed walled up. The locksmiths push in spoon tips, syringe points. So she chooses the opposite attitude: mouth open, gaping, indifferent, jaw hanging, she plays dead, the predator will be repulsed. I pour a spoonful of water, then a second. The water stays in the bowl, the mouth remains gaping. I say: 'close your mouth'. The mouth closes. I say 'swallow'. A pause. A pause. Finally the mouth swallows. My mother stays far away from this scene. The mouth waits. When it is full of water the swallowing reflex is unleashed.

At first the terrible stops being terrible and becomes familiar. One accepts the alteration. Then one forgets. I do not want to forget.

Forget nothing

The last passage from one to the other (my mother and me-hermother) takes place Sunday, 30 June, at 11 o'clock at night, after the nurse has left. I pour some water in her mouth. Then I must have said: 'sleepy time Maman dear' or else 'my love', I no longer know exactly.

I want to keep everything

She marked the page of *Germe* with a piece of Kleenex. But how to keep that, that bit of Kleenex? Date it? I leave it at page 74. Last page.

I want to keep the pain of not having known how to help Ève the least badly possible, I say to my daughter. The word *help* is before me like the orphan cry, the secret name of rescue and she didn't help me translate it. She obeyed me and I was trying to obey her. She didn't know what she needed to say to me she wanted to say to me and didn't know what, she asked me to help her to know what she wanted to ask me to do so that I help her to know what she wanted me to do to help her and I was looking for how to obey her. As she clung to me, I say to my daughter, leaning on my arm she held onto me as if to the force of life, I say, leaning on my daughter. Leaning. Yet another haunting, vacillating word.

In the end I couldn't help her body. The only merciful relation: I would clean her bottom quickly and well, the nimblest, lightest, most agile of gestures, towelette, pants, so that she could return as soon as possible to the refuge without arms without hands of her iron bed.

While she was held up vertically by the nurse, a difficult moment because being inert and abandoned she had the weight of a statue. Everyone suffered, in the back, in the heart, in the soul, and my mother from the bedsore on her sacrum that was turning red like a forge.

The horizon of my existence is this corporal volume prey to fissures, peeling away of the skin, flayings, upheavals of clotted blood, abrasions. I cut off the leaves of skin with paper scissors. It can't be turned on its side because the shoulder is wounded. Layers of cushions are stacked up to keep it on one hip or the other to try to ease the back.

But in December 2012 she is still standing with the help of her cane and leaning on my arm.

I want to keep everything

17 July 2013

Arcachon. In this house, she is not dead, to be sure she is not in her room, but she is not far, there are her flowers, her books, there is still more of still more, she will be on the balcony, all her things are very alive, the mess in the armoire is Ève to a T, cardboard boxes on which she wrote 'pants', full of socks covered with the dust that she will have respected for years, no one else but her.

I no longer know when or how the thought occurred to me that, in Maman's absence, my friend M. could spend a few days in Ève's room, the only bedroom in the house that has a small bathroom. I don't know who had this idea and suggested I adopt it. I could never have had this idea myself. But sometimes I try out the idea of another person. It may be that Ève herself, or her sister Éri, had this idea. But barely arrived, I see the impossibility. Ève is in her room. One doesn't 'see' her, but one sees her in another way. Diffusely. Myself, I hear her call me as soon as I pass in front of the open door, she is not the one who had this idea, Ève at ninety-five years old wearing walking shoes is, among all the èves, the oldest and the most recent, the most helpless, the smallest, the most tenuous, I hear her call me faintly, she hastens me to remember her, I could forget her, she barely moves her eyes she half-opens the wrinkled traits of her lips. –What happened to you, my beloved, I exclaimed, what destitution.

Sleep for a little while yet, I say, it is very early. I will come bring you *Café-au-lait* at 8 o'clock. *Caféaulait* is the drink that consoles her, the milk from a breast that my mother sucks, it is even *the* breast. I pour it by spoonful in her mouth, and each mouthful is visibly a response and a pact. Cat Philia slips into Ève's armoire as usual. The world is open.

How did I ever believe that I could cut away from my heart's flesh the room that is Maman? Did I believe?

Now I am wondering if this room will ever cease being Maman, when? It resists. It does not want to die. This refusal happens when dying enters the house. To not want to die is not to live, it is to remain lying on one's back in the boat, head raised so as to keep watch. –Rest, I say, I am going to stand watch.

This room in the house that is Ève does not cause suffering. It is stronger than us, faithful, a little old but tenacious. The house that is she preserves with a calm stubbornness all the things and bits of string that prove she reigned. The wooden plank for cutting bread has transmitted for forty years the imperial order of her hand: '*remove the crumbs before pushing the plank back in*'. All the rooms speak through edicts displayed on the boxes or in the chalk felt-tip pen on the doors, the walls, in the cupboards. '*No sand in the bathtub / Flush the toilet please / Take out the rubbish on Wednesday / Turn off the electricity / Spin cycle 450*'. She lived surrounded by a people who were always forgetting the essential, a negligent and lazy tribe. She was a house that insisted on being clean, welcoming, tidy. The notices got old, were fly-spotted and mouldy. Looked like the skin of her last face. Strange self-portraits. No one read them any longer. Except me. I look at them with a philosophical devotion. How to think about this transfigurative art. The last sketches were drawn with a powerful brush but trembling all over, the capital letters shiver. Close. Spectres of Ève, as ineffective, as headstrong as the prophets. She believed in humanity since that was all there was, human-ity, with a rational and compulsive naïveté with which god counted on the creatures in whom he had no confidence.

–Stop giving advice, I say. She gives hundreds of pieces of advice and in vain. Then, tired, she comes to ask my advice. –Hélène, what must I do? Too old.

Alas, Hélène does not know the advice.

20 February 2013

–Hélène! Can you explain to me? What am I doing?

–You want to read?

–No.

–You want to sleep?

–Yes. Hélène what could I do?

–I don't know what you could do.

–Me neither.

–What are you thinking about?

–I'm waiting. What are you doing for me?

–I gave you something to sleep.

I adore you. And do you love me?

–I love you very much.

Hélène! What does one do in order to sleep?
–Forget. Don't forget.
–Who forgets?
–Me.
–*What will happen?*

21 February 2013
–Itscares me. What is happening to me?
–Old age. One goes to school and one is a bad pupil. There is no lesson. One doesn't learn anything. One learns nothing.

Law: she never leaves the house without having first made her bed. Commentary: if she has an accident and she is brought back home, everything must be clean and in order for the strangers to see. Commentary on the commentary: she will be brought back home because she took care to note her address and phone number inside her backpack and on the neck of her cane. But now she no longer makes her bed. All the same the address remains on the cane

Psychopathology of Everyday Life

Behaviours: last summer, the last summer, I say to myself, in this disqualified, pale, devitalised summer, before going to sleep, in 2012 I would go downstairs toward her room to lend an ear like a warden who makes sure that his guest is still there. From afar I would hear her making noises, her semi-complaints, her vocalisings in the other language, the language of distress. Then I would go back upstairs.
In Paris in the house of exile, in my name, in this 2013 she made no noise. Where did it go that anxious monologue? Before closing the doors for the night I would go in the dark as far as her regular breathing. In my dream she was sitting in the front seat, silent, I was in the back seat and I was talking politics keenly with the woman driver. Maman didn't move. I would listen for a moment. Then I would go to bed. I don't know why I went like that.
Was I drinking a mouthful of her breath? She was there, silent.
I lived with a breath.

I am running. It's a lost day, late, somewhere in May, that I learn from Victoire that there is no *warning sign*. Sometimes one receives a letter from the authorities three days before departure. Sometimes one will have received nothing. One will not have said Adieu! *Vale!* Until later! I will not be long! You will wait for me? I keep you. You know. You know very well. Keep us. I am waiting for you. I learn from Violette (the nurse with the violet eyes is named Violette, life will have had some fairy-tale aspects in the 2013 reality) that often those who are leaving wait to be alone to do that. That gives rise to more than one explanation. Maman would never do that, I exclaim. The other time she asked me not to go away, I say. It would be a shame if you were not there, she would say. I stayed, and she did too. But that other time, not long ago, she was another. Now she doesn't know when it's time, sometimes she waits on the platform for hours and no time is the right time. In the end any time is perhaps the time or a completely other time.

I'm afraid. I'm afraid of the hour that lasts only a second. I'm afraid of the stolen second: it is extratemporal. It arrives too late, after it has passed.

I am on the edge of Time like a fisherman, I watch my line. One must stop sleeping. Nothing sets the hour apart from other hours. How to recognise it? It's a second of oblivion. The wink of an hour. In truth it's the one that doesn't take place. I imagine that it produces all the same a little sign of recognition. I want to seize the eclipse. I scrutinise. I don't know what. Every instant is the same. Perhaps, a bubble, a roll of foam thin as a thread a note of interrogation, an eyelid that flutters, a word, ah! the idea of a word makes me tremble, she is going to say: ....

and with her difficulty pronouncing, she will swallow half of it, she will mumble a word but chopped up, equivocal, like when she said to me 'goobye' one night, she will say a goobye – and for eternity my viaticum will be an enigmatic diamond, but if I am leaning over her lips at the moment of the word, the movement of the folds, something in her eyes and the whole context, the circumstances, the time, the light, all that will help me guess the sense of the last word, more or less, I must stop sleeping, I must be on alert, alert, not only at night, but also during the day. One doesn't think about it, during the day one believes one is awake and that is the most pernicious illusion, quite mad whoever relies on it. A foreign sleep tries to hoodwink me. I leap up. I run.

In Arcachon 5 August 2013 I hear myself saying to Violette on Sunday, 30 June 2013, at 8 o'clock in the evening: –This afternoon Ève went *Ah!*, it was not a cry, it was not a word, it was a kind of unheard-of term, *Ah!*, I go and I interrogate Violette about this *Ah!* foreigner, as if from another language. Then it comes back to me that the night before, my mother went *Ah! Ah!* around 5 o'clock, but it's the third *Ah!* that holds my attention, it seems to me that it means –*Ah?* says Violette. –Yes, *Ah!* I say. –No, says the nurse. On this gentle Monday of the first of August without Ève's noise, suddenly this *Ah!* rises among the pines. This time I hear it clearly. I am in the state of the grief of Charlemagne who does not hear himself hear Roland's cry, it's an hallucinatory doubtful, dreadful, dreadfully gentle *Ah!* One hears it the time that it is too late.

I'm ruminating on my ruin, I say to my daughter. Those are Ève's rhymes, says my daughter. It's Shakespeare's ruin, I say.

Man wird so alt wie ein Kuh / doch lernt man immer zu, Maman rhymes.

I look up *Ah!* in Shakespeare's sonnets, and I find them, the first sob of sonnet LXVII, *Ah! what wealth she had / In days long since, before these last so bad.*

The last day, there remains *Ah! Ah!* how grave and profound and empty is this Ah, like a *glas,* a knell

Gl   Ah

Such a poverty seizes me suddenly, strikes me, that all the human beings who surround me do not suffice to fill the hole that Maman left in her place in my body–soul. She had become as old as a cow and that did not suffice to know what to want to do how. One learns nothing in advance. I look at the cats with the avidness of one dying of thirst. Living diamonds they eat, they drink, they demand, they proffer their demand profusely. I owe them my survival, this Tuesday of the desert of July 2013.

I go into her room on 31 July, the last day of our last month on earth, and she is not the first to greet me, she does not utter her little cry, she always began and this beginning is finished. I look with all my strength at everything that I do not see. Her Shade raises its head and I say: Maman! But alas I say 'Maman' with the shade of a voice, as if I didn't dare to offend its silence. So I start again, I pronounce 'Maman' a little louder, but the fear of hearing the roar of reality holds me back. Thus is extinguished by me the most tender and the most familiar word in my history. Death cuts my throat, I think. That is exactly the thought that causes Shakespeare's sonnet LXVII to tremble. There exist thoughts that are *like a death*. Merely like. Tomorrow I will try to *say Maman while entering* the room, before the shade falls upon me, I say to myself. I don't want to lose you, you too

Every morning of this February, before 5 o'clock, I go to the shore to see if I am still myself or if half of me has been carried off during my brief sleep. But on the morning of 14 February I go without any doubt: she will be there. She is there. Herself? The same? I don't know. A dusting of *Unheimlichkeit* imbues the air. Victoire, gently certain, me certain rather of the opposite. Later I will think perhaps we make up but one single gentle uncertain certainty, gentle double certainty, duplicitous, for I could doubt since Victoire did not doubt in my place. In February Ève drinks, eats a little enough, *pipi*, *caca*, large wounds, one stops being frightened, we put on the patches, I cut off with office scissors the large pieces of bloody skin, Ève wants to sleep, sleeps, deeply, for weeks, four to eight weeks, April is in another county, H. incredulous. There is a world there that I do not know, it's the world of superhumans, they walk in the mountains of ice for weeks, no human would survive it, they become impossible, they move like dead men that death has not had time to take aboard. Philia, under my left hand, yelps, from this world. A bird goes by. A sleep overwhelms me. With a superhuman effort I get up. Is this Ève's sleep beneath the ice? What is it, this time, unlived, this drifting? In the morning, when we put Ève on the chamber pot, we lift up her block of a body, Roro exclaims: 'Oh she peed on my foot!' Meanwhile standing behind this heavy collapsing body, I have in my right hand a well-formed stool. Another peeps out, which I remove, the way one brings out a newborn. Laughter seizes us, shakes us, we are there, all three of us, Pietà 2013, *pipicaca*, actresses of the natural extremity of carnal life, death's midges, we laugh wholeheartedly, we see ourselves seized, eaten alive by Villon's testament, on seeing myself in Roro and Roro in me, I laugh until I weep and my courage returns, there is some good in misfortune, rorolaughs I laugh at my double, the mirror reflects me larger fatter more astonished, and twice loving, we don't know why we are laughing so hard above the beloved body that predicts that we will fall to pieces. It's because Nature is playing with us, pushing us on the swing above the abyss

but in the afternoon anguish breaks out, Maman whispers in English *Toolate* in uninterrupted flurries, we think that the storm is going to exhaust itself, but the pause opens onto a stronger flurry in French: *Troptard*, what are you doing for me, helpmeehelpmee the voice maddens, pleads, insists, flogs, do do –Tell me, I say while the groaning continues, do you want something to make you sleep? –I want no I want –What do you want? –I don't know, do it for me, forget. *Troptard*
Toolate! Toolate! Toolate!
Forget me Hélène
I have forgotten

What am I doing? What are you doing?

Hélène! Dearest! *Troptard!* Hélène Toolate

An enormous will want wants wants does not know what it wants, insists on not knowing, holds to wanting not to want to know what is going to happen, *what will happen, will, will, will,* says my mother.

And if I thought to accompany my mother toward the exit toward which she insists on not knowing what she wants me to do what I want to know what she wants, if you can't tell me, tell me in English?

Unfortunately fortunately the suspicion is deeply rooted that I am misled and thus that we are all misled, misleading each other. It drives its harpoon into my heart and pulls, pulls.

I am afraid of taking the wrong road, and I take the wrong road, I say to Victoire, an inadequate expression, there is no other road, but all the same adequate, as if I were swallowing truth the wrong way, whereas Victoire is firm in her positions, she cannot recover, she says, I agree, we are recovering the wrong way, I remain firm in my uncertainties that my mother dictates to me on the one hand in the morning, on the other hand in the evening. Thus every morning I think that Victoire is mistaken. Every evening I think that what she says is right. I advance without gaining any distance, while limping, in a foreign obscurity, I recognise no one, except the cats, between two contrary miracles, life, death, which are absolutely indissociable. Life makes the dead woman, death stirs restlessly. The shade Death splashes on everything that moves, my two cats pass by at a gallop. I will extinguish you two as well.

Life, death, senseless, incomprehensible phenomena. Why, why? says my mother. No response. Why does *It* stop, why does It all stop, why does itallstop. No reason. Except the discouragement of the subject. The soul is intact. It takes leave in English. *Goodnight!*

Life: in the morning from 7 o'clock to noon. Ève sneezes far away. A pistol shot. The cats jump. I hasten. What if? Wide awake, charming: 'Maman-Maman!' She wants Maman not Omi, that means she's come back a few steps on the invisible road. I cover her up, turn on the light, death vanishes.

Victoire comes early. –Jam! Ève says in triumph. There! She wants and her wanting has an object that had been scrapped. I hurry, accompanied by a little bit of shame. I had believed that Jam was in the past. Ève swallows two little spoonfuls of jam. We congratulate her. I learn a lesson in jam on 23 February. If the idea, the desire for jam are revived, from there … . A sacred halo radiates around the apricot preserves in the refrigerator. It could resuscitate.

What am I doing there? Leaning toward my mother I lend an ear.
I see myself. The breath that I gather in seems to come from very far
away. One has to imagine a sort of telephone conversation between two
psyches separated by an unimaginable distance within proximity itself.
I want to question the other. I hesitate. Will I say: where are you? That
would suppose she hears me. Or will I say to myself: where is she? She
would have lost her way in a city to which she was drawn, perhaps by
the urgency of looking for someone she left behind and whose presence
or absence she regrets. So she will be in Osnabrück or Strasbourg, and
feverish, hurried by the danger, she speaks to the passers-by, to the air,
she asks for her mother, she calls: Omi! In a tone that is distressed,
sorrowful, a little ashamed. It's because it's been so long since she has
called her. Oh yes, she had forgotten her, and now here is the time when
she will need Omi. It's because tomorrow she is going back to school,
a totally unknown world, and she went to bed all dressed so as not to
be surprised by a delay, this night is the last night of this past life. And
it's the first time that she cannot pass from one life to another without
Omi giving her her hand. She has come back to the point of departure.
Now she half-opens her eyes but just barely, is it a gaze? Or is it a quick
withdrawal of the gaze? She says, somewhere, in the empty immensity
of the bedroom, or perhaps into the telephone mike: 'Omi', or 'Omi?'
She asks herself for Omi, I say to myself. Or else she asks herself: is that
you, Omi? So it is time to get up and go to school. Very softly, then, so
as not to spoil the least vital illusion, I lower my voice, I take all colour
out of it, I mask it with a veil of distance and

I murmur: 'Yes! *Ich bin hier. Omi ist da.*'

My mother nods her head. It means: 'I know that you are not Omi but
that you are Omi all the same. Good night, Omi!'

'She called you Omi!' exclaims my daughter. She too is receiving the
coded telegram. It's the first time.

The day is approaching for going to school the first time. The day
when one is going to lose one's mother for the first time.

I am in the process of losing the long happiness, I say to myself.

This day defeated me. I say to myself, 17 February.

Is it because Ève said Omi to me several times?

Thus Omi has entered this story. But who is this Omi? Is it her
mother, forgotten remembered forgotten? Is it death? Is it the ancestor
left in Osnabrück at the beginnings of her memory?

–All of a sudden I understand *L'Arrêt de Mort*, I say to my daughter.
The dying woman who stops death, repels it, holds it under her fist, for
a long time, before getting tired. It's a battle. My mother is looking for
weapons, ammunition. Life my mother. It will have been Ève herself, life

itself. Trust itself. Gathering up all the enormous energies of a baby she is looking for something. She finds it: jam.

I keep turning things over. I use my daughter to turn things over. I cannot believe, I say. Cannot. Cannot swallow. Want to vomit the death jam. Powerful I am without force and without power, I could do anything but what do you want, Ève is watching, I watch over her sleep, how to keep watch without sleeping, sleep I am watching I say to her. Hypervigilance, says my daughter, that is precisely the sign. Jam! exclaims my mother. Happiness in desiring a thing that one can obtain, that responds. Thus death takes on the features of life, or it's life that sweeps death away with a word, one lives with all one's strength. One cries: I am here! Don't believe it!

But already the poison insinuates itself, by a turn of phrase, worms its way into a thought expression. Why do I say that I cannot believe? As if I were defending myself. As if believing were already there, but without me.

I note nothing in March 2013, in my white notebook, it's as if I wasn't able to confide to the white notebook Ève's unbelievable decline. The fright is for the red Venice notebook where I store away the anxious observations of the commander of the *Unheimlich*: Today 5 March, it's as if for four days she has abandoned hope. Right away in the morning, for greeting: Toolate. Then: Lost. Then: Past. Hurt? Everywhere. This little red notebook films our path. Without it I will not be conscious of the journey. The path of ice has an infinite elasticity.

Life gives way by millimetres, by days as thin as a knife blade. This wear is imperceptible.

A gloomy week, without exchange. Fortunately *caca pipi*. Not a word. We say to ourselves *all is lost*. I think of nothing but her death. Until Tuesday, 12 March, when, inexplicably, speech returns. And at the same time, *the courage* that I had lost. At 9 o'clock in the morning she says: –Hélène! help me. I was under a tent of ice. I jump up, galvanised. Ève is winning! She is there! H. –What do you want? È. –Give me a kiss. I cover her in kisses: forehead, hollow cheeks. Then the unlocatable mouth, caved in, but kissed. She responds awkwardly. I incite her. –You too! A kiss. She forms a vague kiss. She has never kissed. Kissing is French. A hundred years without kissing, and suddenly. È. –A little more. I kiss her ardently. Enough now. È. –A little cuddling. And there's a word she has never pronounced. If one could nourish her with kisses and cuddling, she could very well live.

On 15 March, the darkness is there.

Two sentences. In the evening, in front of Violette the nurse: –It's grave. In the morning to Roro: –Why does no one help me? Why don't I believe? Toolate. *Roro.* –Too late what? *È.* –Too old Toolate Enough I've enough.

An explosion of Toolate. *H.* –What can I do? *È.* –Find the strength. (*A pause. Explosion.*) Ne-cessary.

A pause. Bad blood.

Thus do we go, in the gusts, variations of darkness, I have the keys but I don't see the door, truths strike, Ne-cessary! then withdraw. An angry crowd of feelings. She doesn't know what to do! Stones fly. Flight of stones in the darkness.

At 8 o'clock morning and evening I give her the shot of calciparine, she lets me do it, in the morning she says: 'Help me,' in the evening she says: 'Toolate.'

Necessary challenges me, scoffs at me. One is not departing, all of a sudden one is departing again. One certainty: nothing happens as one thought. Ève is immortal. This immortality blocks, crosses out, erases in advance the coming months, sometimes letting only a little life go on, sometimes letting a little life pass.

I am agonising in the little dimly lit hallway.

Then one morning in April, the 4th, although nothing particular, the little familiar quiver of *life*, indubitable life, like victory-life, joy life, weak but clear like a first bird song in spring, although: no spring, no bird, glacial April. Only the motivation. Life that shakes itself all alone, without reason, merely out of love for itself. Purrs. Philia on my left hand, same game: purrs. I have been loved, I thought. Then I think with love of my beloveds, of Ève, tenacious, funny, who foils all the calculations, lives lives lives, opens her beak, chirps, opens an eye, meows, does what she can, when she can, sails in her Medicalisedbed, loses all at once, all that one can lose, the essence of time, of place, of reason, of orientation, of the self, of presence, of the shore, of direction and yet keeps, keeps the need not to lose, the strength to not want to want to struggle no longer to take up the old bit of life that she left on her night table soaking in a glass of water while she herself plunged into the bottomless well beneath sleep.

Sometimes when I bring her back up out of the well she no longer has the strength to repay the climb with a word. But on 5 April, like the character who slept a hundred years, upon coming out of the cavern she is concerned to know what the world is up to. She hastens with an acute sense of reorganisation: Who am I? Where am I? Who are you? Who is that? Where we going? I answer without hesitation. All the boxes ticked. 'That's good,' says Ève, and she is at peace like the God who has verified his weekly accounts and everything adds up.

So I push god in ruins in the wheelchair toward the window. –Do you see the tulip? A big tulip. Ève doesn't look. Doesn't see. I turn her head a little in the right direction. –What colour is the tulip? –Red. –That's good.

On 16 April it's the end of the world in colour. Ève, shrivelled, sagging, reduced to two words: 'I'm afraid.' At those words I become afraid. Then everything passes. We take up again something that is neither courage nor hope, a kind of alliance, after a very serious storm, we thought it was the end and then we find ourselves again rolling and pitching in the dark hallway, and terror spreads its flattened shadow behind us.

27 July 2013

Then little by little her bedroom will fade. She will no longer greet
with the words of Maman and her voice that age has rusted when I enter
in the early morning hours *bonjour!* is it time for *café au lait*? No, it's
too early it's 5 o'clock sleepy time, thank you, and she will no longer
docilely close her large eyelids, to obey the ritual. I will have to repel
the rapid sprout of nothingness with the help of prostheses, to stop up
the walls overtaken by the void with patches of photographs, but which
ones, who is going to pass through this room, which Ève, who is going
to deposit on the wicker chair that has followed my mother since 1934
in all her exiles its confused heap of jackets sweaters bathrobes, I do not
know which one will detach itself from the hundred shadows, which
one will be exchanged for which other, the time of a vision, I have had
so many and loved so many, and each one arrives with its rapid, firm,
wobbling, decomposed step to present its love services, is it I who will
smooth out your heart, the one who would go to the market as if into
battle, is it I the goddess who saved you from fiery exile, the beautiful
and beneficent star who appeared on that Sunday when you were nine
years old and you were crouching in a jail of solitude, is it the one who
struggled without conviction against mad violinist lovers and whom I
had to get out of trouble, is it the sixth Ève, the one who expelled from
Algiers one Tuesday night began to reconstruct a shelter on Wednesday
with Omi on her back, having carried with her only a backpack and her
midwife notebooks in which were sleeping unleavened the two hundred
and forty newborns by Easter, is it the rebeginner on the ruins, is it the
one who brought death down with bludgeon blows, because she had the
strength of a demi-god in her arms, is it the one with whom I brought
out without pain and without doctor my three children from my interior
pocket? No
it comes to me at the edge of my heart that the one whom I want to find
again safe and sound is the old Ève proud of her exploits and the exploit

was not a great deed from one of her wars, but having leaped over the frontier of very old age while leaning on the stick of her umbrella and to crown her victory having gone with me and my friends from the Kleber book shop to swallow, gobble, get down a sauerkraut for champions, at the Kammerzell in Strasbourg, being then *uralt*, sparkling super-old, ninety-two years after having left her native city to leave room for the little French girls who would dance on the tables that had just been put away by the little German girls including herself, when on that day in 1918 the little Klein girls were very hungry and my mother had had the right to a soup of Quaker Oats distributed by American charity to the starving Germans. To eat to live will have always been a religious and measured act watched over by Ève.

I want my old woman. Her way of signing her familiar messages 'I am going to miss you my dearest darling, Ève Cixous,' first name last name, as if over time she had made a name or a first name for herself identifying her perhaps as the author of those imponderable sculptures of life, *Hic fuit Ève Cixous*. As if someone in her had stood up to occupy the place of curator of her humble traces. Or else as if she had arrived in such a foreign country that every day she had to recall where she came from, that she was a woman née Klein in Germany who, afterwards, had become Ève Cixous in Algeria, as if she had to fill out every day certificates of life, because her existence could be put in doubt by the authorities. Her inexhaustible source of acquiescence to everything that I proposed to her, as if she loved me like herself, which simplified her life a lot. –Are you coming? To the park, to Chicago, to Umea, to Lund, to Frankfurt, to Madrid, to the ocean, to the Bonnard exhibit, to the demonstration, to the theatre, to vote. –Yes. –To Algiers. –Algiers? Without me.

I am waiting for her in front of the door to the building, she is coming back up the Samuel Beckett walkway while wavering, accompanied in a first period by her umbrella in the role of a cane, in a second period by her cane that becomes her third leg, her portable daughter the apple of her eye, even her mother.

–How can one love so passionately, in such a particular way, an old used-up woman? Bouvard and Pécuchet ask me.

I hope you are recovering slowly from the loss of dear Ève, hope Bouve and Pecuche in English, on 1 August 2013, things are better after a month, we read that in Freud, *says Bouve*. Note the modalising *slowly*, that changes everything, *says Pecuche*. I translate: 'I hope you are recovering *lentement* from the loss.' Yes, yes. Thank you, says Ève. Okay? Yes okay. *De profundis clamavi* It's okay.

My voice cries famine. I want to feel the taste of the word Maman in my mouth, I want to eat the sun, I want to swallow it, I want to sing you a song.

But little by little her bedroom will fall silent. But let all the singers of the testament come to my aid. I laugh at and live on Villon, I announce his will to the will of my old woman.

Just as Omi is nothing any longer, except for her representation in a frame. But the image is not nothing. Yet it is only a face, a cut-off head, but in this one elegant image are concentrated the rich volumes of a life, with its dramas, its journeys, its Europes and its Africas, its odysseys of the German woman in French, there is in the launching force of the gaze something like a monumental warning of an Omissey. A poet would suffice to give text to this fragment.

As if there remained of Shakespeare only two lines, three, in which would be condensed the energy, the promise, of a hundred thousand poems, these lines would have the force of the fire of Prometheus, they would cause humanity to dream

I will write a letter to the mayor of Osnabrück.
Lieber Herr Wolfgang Griesert,
The last spark of the Jonas (Meyer, Klein) family ... Es tut mir Leid, I am sorry to inform you, it hurts me and all the more pain-fully still that I do not dare continue my sentence in German since my mother is no longer here to watch over the correction of my grammar.

Little by little the city of Osnabrück, in which I have lived, in a bor-rowed reality called up by the many stories protected by the warm voice of my mother from the attacks of time, a busy life, whether sometimes at Omi's home sometimes at the home of her friends, always with a pleasure sharpened by curiosity regarding as many characters as there are in the *Iliad*, and all having at first a prosperous, industrious, optimistic exist-ence, with in view exciting prolongations on other continents, realisable dreams, stories of marriages with incalculable outcomes, fodder for Dr Freud, commercial relations and sometimes banking connections with Kafka the son, then brutally e-lim-i-na-ted from Osnabrück, at short intervals, kicked out, dispossessed, gone astray, terrified, massacred, separated, turned into the miserable wretches of cruel novels, bitter, abandoned, forgotten, persons banished from the realm of memory, poor people, spiritual beggars, atrophied ones, badly adopted ones who no longer ever think of Osnabrück, the city of Osnabrück would cease to resuscitate, little by little I will not be able to return there with delight, mother Homer is dead

little by little onto this world as beautiful and populous as the London of 1599 and as pregnant with the seeds of the centuries will descend a sheet of fog and I will no longer manage to find the entrance to it,

I will no longer remember my grandmother's address, I will have lost the phone number of my great-grandmother Hélène Meyer, I will no longer remember her name

They say that 'It' passes. Death begins and recovers very *slowly*, it takes years and that's the process. Mother Homer is dead ...

but perhaps I will have the good luck, the right, to leave before the end

On Sunday, 28 April, as I survey the traces of these last weeks, I see with stupefaction the incessant turnarounds of my moods, it's a kind of mournful *fort-da*, the way I do not stop going toward death, accepting it, wanting it, dismissing it, believing, not believing, covering every day the narrow path on the edge of the abyss, saying my farewells, for nothing, and each time kaleidoscopings of the times that are coming, scenarios that pile up, cancel each other, mutate, one time I add to Maman's death the death of Philia, I take the bodies of Ève and my cat together to the cemetery the pain is so great that I cry 'god, don't take my cat from me, not the cat!' and I add to the horror a list of losses that I will not name, whereupon the brevity, the narrowness, the crevice, summer, summer, lethe, the it-was [*l'été, l'été, léthée, l'était*] of the dozens of dead summers present themselves, throw me a burnt-up wink and internally I turn every six hours toward the opposite, impaled as I am on the spit of time, sickening churning, severe cancellation of all affects, tachycardias, vertigos, low blood pressure, a laugh a week, gags over the mouth, sudden terrors, repressed sobs. And dreams swollen with the dead and cemeteries.

In the middle of the sorrows a sentence of Jean Santeuil comes and goes: *but the thoughts that had awakened in her went back to sleep again in vain, she was unable to make them be as if they had not been.*

A bus route, Thought-of-death, round-trip, the one my mother would often take in dream.

It occurs to me that my mother was undergoing at the same time as me the same bad weather, but that each one of us being isolated in her heart I never knew if she was in fact coming back when I believed she was going away or conversely.

At the end of the afternoon I have the overwhelming impression that Ève is leaving. I tie myself to her bed, I caress her cold cheeks, I kiss her lipless mouth, an inert crack, no strength to talk, a few breaths come out in puffs –What? I say. Are you saying 'goodbye'? I say, trying to bring a disarticulated murmur to the edge of a meaning. It could be 'à boire', *drink*, but it's 'auoir', *goobye*. Finally I incline to believe that she wants me to leave, Anne and I are perhaps making too much noise, this account that cascades above the abyss that she is, but I don't want *auoir*, I have ears only for the breath, if it was the secret, if I missed it, if Toolate had taken power, if I arrived a glance too late, ah! if I deprived my life of the last ray, forever my eyes would be lifeless, I am at the edge of my mother's bed like a frightened lover, convinced at the bottom of my primitive soul that my fate, my survival, are decided by the last instant, the one that either gives us the slip or pardons us, the last judgment, the sentence: you were there, life, you were not there, you will never again find the house of the beyond. For I am part of that mystical free masonry that gambles its right to eternity on a glance.

At that moment, Ève *raises* her eyelids (for she needs the weak forces of mind to raise the curtain again) and *casts* a little colourless glance to the side. Alas, this is not a letter. What is undeniable and cruel for my heart: at that moment she is alone, is not turned toward me, does not respond, wants: nothing. If *it* was in that instant, *it* would be sadly without farewell. Want: *auoir*.

'What is certain', says my daughter, 'is that she is no longer on the side of the living.'

Now we wander in this foreign country where one encounters strict and senseless sentences. So I think: I must find out right away how one goes to the side that is the other side where my mother is still living. I cannot believe that she left me or that I left her without this being signified to me.

For my daughter there is an it's-certain. I vacillate, no it's-certain is held out to me. For such a long time I have been slowly flying wide-eyed in the void between two invisible shores. I note: my daughter's calm who is 'out in front' of me. I 'lag' behind with little Ève.

It does me good that my daughter whom I revere puts an it's-certain before me like a little plank on which to set down for a fraction of a second my dismembered spirit. It reassures me that there exists in the ravaged world some perches, some benches, some fords in the river, the idea of sides, the possibility of distinguishing, dear beings with calm voices whereas I quake and my mother creaks and squeals. What-is-certain becomes a tree in the tornado that whirls me about. At least someone whom I love stands like a mast in the chaos. However this poor old shrivelled love in me has eyes only for the old life that provides me with life. Fear of letting it go, that she will let me go, fear of losing the last drop of blood. Thus I still wait for her to give to me. She gives me what she has left: nothing. Goes away very slowly, detached, indifferent. She doesn't call me. So that's it? It's there? We are dead perhaps? Perhaps in the middle of the Lethe. When one is in the middle of the river, one doesn't know, one floats.

We are floating.

'And this, what is this?' says Roro. 'Tu-? Tu-?'

Ève-that-remains is wedged in the wheelchair among five cushions, a cushion under her knees, a cushion under her nape, her neck bent, her head cut off on her shoulder, cushions under her arms, moaning helpme. Roro says: 'Tu-?' Waits for Ève to complete the tu-. 'Tulips!' Hélène laughs. *Roro:* –Where? Where? Where? *Ève weak:* –Park. Roro delighted, her champion has won. Suddenly enters the sparkling idea of a walk in the park. Suddenly I have a radiant vision of us in the park. I hold onto it with all my strength. I greet it. And what if we arrived at the Park?

Then vision of a book with three pages of helpmee. At least *one* page. It is necessary. Otherwise no one will be able to imagine the music of this glacial time.

helpmee   helpmee   helpmee   helpmee   helpmee
helpmee   helpmee   helpmee   helpmee   helpmee
helpmee   helpmee   helpmee   helpmee   helpmee
helpmee   helpmee   helpmee   helpmee   helpmee
helpmee   helpmee   helpmee   helpmee   helpmee
helpmee   helpmee   helpmee   helpmee   helpmee
helpmee   helpmee   helpmee   helpmee   helpmee
helpmee   helpmee   helpmee   helpmee   helpmee
helpmee   helpmee   helpmee   helpmee   helpmee
helpmee   helpmee   helpmee   helpmee   helpmee
helpmee   helpmee   helpmee   helpmee   helpmee
helpmee   helpmee   helpmee   helpmee   helpmee
helpmee   helpmee   helpmee   helpmee   helpmee
helpmee   helpmee   helpmee   helpmee   helpmee
helpmee   helpmee   helpmee   helpmee   helpmee
helpmee   helpmee   helpmee   helpmee   helpmee
helpmee   helpmee   helpmee   helpmee   helpmee
helpmee   helpmee   helpmee   helpmee   helpmee
helpmee   helpmee   helpmee   helpmee   helpmee
helpmee   helpmee   helpmee   helpmee   helpmee
helpmee   helpmee   helpmee   helpmee   helpmee
helpmee   helpmee   helpmee   helpmee   helpmee
helpmee   helpmee   helpmee   helpmee   helpmee
helpmee   helpmee   helpmee   helpmee   helpmee
helpmee   helpmee   helpmee   helpmee   helpmee
helpmee   helpmee   helpmee   helpmee   helpmee
helpmee   helpmee   helpmee   helpmee   helpmee
helpmee   helpmee   helpmee   helpmee   helpmee
helpmee   helpmee   helpmee   helpmee   helpmee

Suddenly the cat is limping. Suddenly she hides. Suddenly she disappears. I look for her *everywhere* in vain. A flood of tragic visions abruptly flows, I pour out a flood of heavy tears that my mother drew from my depths. –Enough, death! –But don't you know that death is never satisfied? You thought you had paid with just your father's cadaver? –I thought so, but I got over it

And I had the dream of the disinterment of my father. And this dream was interred, but on 27 April 2013 I managed to disinter it. It's in the room below, which serves as storage, in the corner on the floor a silhouette covered with sheets of paper. Here is where my dead father is stored. Naturally it is out of the question to approach it, to touch it. That is not done. However the idea arises in me that I *must* do it, despite the risks. Risks: of seeing the horror perhaps, of losing him, with no going back. It's already a lot to be able to approach this stretched-out, set-aside body. I don't resist. I want all the same to see Papa. In reality. Too bad for all of you. I lift the paper sheet. And there is the face of the dead man, a little long, emaciated, and as if mummified. He doesn't look much like Papa alive, but he is there, it's a reunion. What a good thing I've done. I kiss this dead face. I even ask to make a photocopy. I am more and more audacious. Will I show it to Maman? I want to keep traces. Look. Look all of you: a long, dry, narrow face, with strange proportions, a knife blade. Eyes closed. Without any expression. Abandonment. But love passes. When I kiss him, I cross through the inexpression. It is as if I *accepted* what death does to us, rather than wanting to hold on to the final beauties. I have dared to cross the limits and I don't regret it. I have seen what one cannot see. What I had not seen. What the dead hide. I feel a cold joy, an internal strength, the joy of the truth. Nothing beautiful. But I did not flee, did not abandon it. This dream was lost, I say to my daughter. Totally. Like all those of that week that harsh Reality steals from me. She says to me: I am more awful and more true than the dreams. But the jolts of despair are stronger. When I had given up, a pity sent it back to me, right before the last death. If I had lost this reunion-with-my-father, pitiless, this dried-up face, if I had lost death, what a misfortune! And I would not even have felt it.

Dead and alive I want Maman.

From 30 April to 6 May, Maman's rhythm being the same, I get into the habit of *passing*: I cocoon, I bend, I crumble, I go away again. In the morning she is there, her eyes present, life. A little nest egg of words, just what is necessary: 'Hélène', 'Drink', 'No'. And a word for luxury and panache: 'Merci'. In the evening she leaves, everything is closed, mouth folded in, tongue folded back, eyes far away, the body run aground, in withdrawal, refusal to respond, saves her breath. Attached to the rhythm, I follow my mother the morning I think I'm alive, the evening I think that she is leaving shutters closed detached from me, leaves without me, me detached from me, I follow her no more, in vain I insist, she *opposes* me with a refusal. Cold cheeks.

Until the month of May, she had never *opposed* me.

The idea that La Boétie could become unattached to him, did it ever visit Montaigne, even for a minute?

On Sunday, 6 May, in the morning, she calls me: '*Mutter!*' It's an honour and a grace. When she called me Omi, it was her little frightened child self that was asking for help from Omi everyone's-mother. *Mutter* is the word used in grave, solemn, decisive circumstances and in which she constitutes a secret union faced with strangers. One word for nothing but two.

On 1 August 2013 it appears to me that during all those months when I didn't know that I was, I was passing so quickly so slowly, I passed myself by, I never thought that I was having an experience of *Unheimlichkeit*, about which I have dreamed written, reflected, I never even thought. *Unheimlichkeit* fell upon me in a few hours on 14 January, naturally in an *unheimlich*, imperceptible or infrahuman way, so that I was suddenly awakened on board the boat of the hunter Gracchus, perhaps in the hold, it was mad, it was a fact, I couldn't explain it to myself, I asked twenty times what had caused such damage and it was a pointless question, what's the good of knowing why one dies. My mother had fallen, nothing broken, a life broken, one has more than one of them, but the replacement life is junk as my mother says. I was still trying to rejoin her, we were in cities swallowed by water, she was just ahead of me and I couldn't find her, I was talking to her and she answered me sideways, as if I was on another side, she herself kept losing me even if I was holding her hand, a kind of moveable blindness enveloped her and separated her from my hand, she wasn't receiving the messages that however a movement of her neck seemed to receive, I said I'mhere so often that this word had become a sort of proper name common to the two of us.

The last Saturday, as I was moving two steps away from the Medicalisedbed, she raised her head which she didn't have the strength to move so as to follow me with her eyes and I didn't see her, my back was turned, it was F & C who alerted me: 'she's looking for you!' I threw myself toward her but already she had lost me. How quickly one loses someone. A fraction of a second, you don't know which one, and you see the gulf where the disappearance occurred. Thus during all those months, I belonged continually to my mother, not an instant to any other, except the cats, and I misplaced her often. I no longer know how many times.

On 20 May, time stopped, I am working on *what happens to us* as fate, to us, beings whom we lose before the end, I'm thinking of you, who died before being dead, Ajax, Catherine Earnshaw. But Ève is not dead. There was an arrest of death, at a certain distance. Death is not in the house, I say to myself, 21 May, although the state of the body is frightful, the soul is steadfast.

We make love, despite the presence of the family, you lean toward me and whisper to me a vital message, very quickly in my ear, I sense that it is the address and the key, it's even the reason that you are making love to me, a pretext to detect the secret, unfortunately you speak softly, I can't hear, what did you say? you murmur a second time, I don't hear, you whisper again and again at the edge of my ear, I don't grasp the *words* but the tender breath of love envelops me. –What are you telling me, Maman? Tell me the word.
   –But there are no more words in the language in which I meow, you understand the cats fine, why don't you understand me? 'I'm doin 'at I 'an 'gain and 'gain.'

Compared to this last insignificant and melancholic day of July 2013, all the days of the year were divided into several months endowed with that duration of a magically convincing century-hour as in films cut from the cloth of dreams. I had barely the time to hold onto them with a few notes. All the days of the year radiated a double brilliance. Each one could have been one of the last days, each one had the poignant seduction of a day that could have been the next-to-last, it could have been the last Saturday before the last Sunday, haloed by the magnifying intensity of what forever belongs to the unique and the solemn, and thus each moment was caught in the strange amber of the event, every day or almost had the impressing power of the apocalypse or of the day before, and in me the mysterious forge of the watch was activated, and everything I did and that happened was simultaneously inscribed and reread, the self that I would be in ten years would relive each day each year in meticulous and melancholic anniversaries, just as each year begins again one summer day, like the song of the thrush that takes Chateaubriand back to all his childhoods, the twenty-sixth song of my round-trip odyssey Arcachon Ithaca Montaigne Ithaca, during which I *relive*, and each year with a sorrow that is a slightly different colour, the last day of our visits to Montaigne, when you wept for the dead man, as if we were in Jerusalem, I would say to you: but he lived a long time and in the eternal splendour of writing, and sitting on the stone bordered with buttercups you inconsolated yourself over finitude, saying that no life escaped brevity, that it runs out of breath in the fifty-ninth year or the hundred and third,

and just as each grain of the stones of the tower and each buttercup entered, I knew it, into the throng of my soul

so every minute of the days that could turn out to have been the very last of my perfect life with my mother came to plant its buttercup brilliance in my condemned soul.

But at the same time once the twenty-first hour of this day subject to fate had been surpassed alive, the hour of the nursing care that pulled the curtain of bandages on this day at sea, I had the mad impression that we were come into port safe and sound, we dropped the anchor of anxiety, a reprieve was granted us for several hours I believed, it's only around 10 o'clock in the morning that the howling wind rose again, something in the defence of Ève's besieged organism was weakening, the height of danger comes at the end of the afternoon. I was always there, I saw nothing, I went round in circles. When she then enters into sleep, we reduce the expenses and the risks, there is a truce, the enemy is also sleeping, and I sometimes wished that she would sleep for a long time a very long time, in that way her life would be prolonged, I could keep her indefinitely like an old sleeping beauty, the Thing not being able to happen except during a daytime attack.

I was wrong. I still have not succeeded in thinking anything about this error, I tell myself today 9 August 2013.

And it never occurred to me that such a life in lethargy was related to the case of Mr Valdemar who died and was dead before himself or else after himself.

I had passed the boundaries, I don't know when, and without noticing it.

Such were the flowers of my thoughts this day of August 2013. I gathered, so as to bring them back to my mother's room, large wild parasol shapes in the fortunately neglected meadow that stretches before Montaigne's Tower where nothing had changed almost everything was once again the same, except my heart, my life, my vision of the world, the images of the years that would come to hollow out and deepen the wound in my soul, now I will return more dead to the Tower, I will be less, I will be half ghost, I will have the spectral bodies of the little one and my mother lodged in my breast I resemble more and more a living cemetery, I say to myself. Whereas Montaigne carried to the end only one body sewn into his flesh.

There are no more stories to tell about me, thinks my mother, I raise my tongue and I lower it. I have nothing. I am called Ève. My daughter is called Hélène. I call her. Hélène! Hélène! I have some word in my mouth, and for nothing. I believe I was born in Heidelberg. Where I have never been. Oran means nothing to me. I am afraid of towers. Too high. I am afraid they will happen to fall on me. I am afraid to sleep and that they fall me. *I want to sleep*. I want Maman.

She was of the world, I say to my daughter, she was right no longer to know whether she was from Osnabrück or Strasbourg, from Paris or Algiers, what does it matter where she began, she has always been a passionate spectator of the life of other people, what interests her everywhere is usefulness.

Catheter? It was perhaps on 30 May? I keep quiet with all my strength. Catheter. The blows rained down, I grit my teeth. I had the impression of a murder. All the more violent and cruel in that it was perpetrated kindly, by innocent beings whom I love. In appearance a little medical formality, in me I was resisting, I was internally on my knees in the final wrath of a bull wounded to death. One feels nothing when it is inserted. And I was ashamed of this self who was thrashing me about in secret like one possessed. It will be more comfortable, yes yes, a discreet act, the consequences of which are beneficial for the woman. One avoids all the inevitable brutality of raising the tortured body to transport it to the toilet-chair, one grants a favourable response to her request for peace in bed. One ought to have 'inserted the catheter' a long time ago because each raising caused another wound. She will be saved from all the rendings and tearings. Catheter rhymes with nothing, Ève would say. But she didn't say any more. She had said yes for Omi, in Omi's place, when she was the daughter, that is to say me. It is the first time we are going to 'do to her' something without her being informed. I would say to her: it's a matter of an 'improvement' that will introduce into the bedroom and into the woman's body at the same time a pacification as a sign of supplementary surrender. But one can also say it the other way around: it's a surrender that brings a paradoxical benefit. And then she would say to me: 'Y'reright.' Still another one of her words forged through fusion. But I say nothing. I cannot consult her. She cannot help me to help my mother.

I was a primitive people who repels the benefits of civilisation then submits, death in my soul, knowing that in order to slow the progress of the destruction it begins by preparing the first ceremony of death.

And there was the apocalypse. And my mother was unveiled.

Ève has always been naked, with the nakedness of a cat, a nakedness before nakedness, without apocalypse. In the time of her long youth and her splendour she was always naked according to her name, with a newborn's nakedness, and since we have been in the time of her misery she has always been of a non-denuded nakedness.

1 June, the day of the break-in, it is not the fact of having witnessed along with the nurse angel the disaffected vision of her sex that makes my heart bleed, it's entering into her vestibule without being able to ask her authorisation. She would certainly not have refused. But we are doing everything in her absence.

It was supposed to be fair weather that evening. I had no eyes for the sky. Maman will never again get up again, I was thinking.

During the movements, she who set moving the stars and my thoughts, *die Wolken, Luft und Winden / Gibt Wege, Lauf und Bahn*, without saying a word she joins the world of defenceless animals. From a large wound on her right arm there escapes in the place of her song a dribble of light red blood.

A thought says: if Ève departs, will have to, putting everything else on hold, write her book. For nothing lasts, this blood is going fade, this song is going to vanish. Unless the worst: the nurse small slender sparkling eyes and an abundance of wisdom says on the telephone: Madame C. is at the end of life. A mad truck crosses the bedroom, passes a centimetre away from Ève's head, swallows in one gulp the bathroom, which was constructed for her toilet and remains as it was for the last ablutions, with her towels ready, her seat where Ève was able to sit her body right before the bedsore, and in a hurricane roar reduces our shelter to rubble. We are administered I say to myself in a flash. The words weigh so heavily that I realise my soul is full of water. It's sinking.

Yesterday, 1 June 2013, I betrayed Maman, me, who at the sight of the opening of the large wound on the right forearm, the third opening of the day, the first was the pocket of blood on the right shoulder, bloodied shirt, the second the crack on the leg, the third then the discovery of bubbles the size of my hand, the flowering nurse and I seal it. Wrapped up like a serious burn victim the body is hidden from my mother's sight. There remain the marbled thighs, I slide among the spots of blood I want to kiss my mother I give her a shot, tomorrow I will have to prick in the haematoma, 'bad blood', says Maman's uneasy soul, the ruins are advancing I am losing courage. Only the left foot resists, wrapped up in sheepskin it testifies that here had been a well-built, agile and indefatigable woman. Meanwhile the deathly fire devours the flesh. And suddenly a fiery cat bites me and plants its claws in my heart, the savage idea that one ought, it is necessary, I want, we want, to end. Enough! Enough seeing Maman overturned on the toilet-chair, the mouth-hole wide open, mute cry, twisted neck, bent nape, arms and legs torn apart, lacerated enough! Flayed enough! cries a broken-necked rage.

I surprise myself: sitting on my bed with the two cats one of my hands as if borrowed from my mother holds my chin. It is Maman's gesture. A part of her supports the collapsing head. The hand supporting my chin is full of the blood of lipstick. My decomposed mother haunts me. What are we doing here? Are we obeying? What? Obeying whom do we disobey whom? We don't kill we kill. Great shame on me who doesn't know how not to betray.

Ève in the time of her splendour
Ève in the time of her misery
I'm afraid
That the one will make me unfaithful to the other.

Do not kill me. What must I do? Everyone asks herself, and me too I ask myself. Do and be quiet.

A year ago she was ready to die with me during the night, one had to do nothing, one goes to sleep and one rejoins Omi at the station, Éri as well if she is not late as usual. Now this self that It did not make laugh but that issued its orders to me with an assurance acquired through a profound psychological apprenticeship as noted in her beautiful large disciplined handwriting, this self of the responsible selfmidwife parturient, who followed without hesitation the watchwords *useful*, '*affective and emotional mobilisation*', was no longer current. The motivation '*one must be interested and convinced by the desire to succeed with and by the parturient*' is now but a dried-up article. It's necessary to start the conditioning again from zero. She forgets that she knew how. One must reprepare oneself. Ève! Ève! One must! One must! She is like a parturient who has already practised painless childbirth and doesn't want to repeat the preparation. Or seek the causes. It can happen that failure is caused by the previous success. In the case of my mother the subject has distanced herself from her determined self. Enthusiasm is necessary. This is a source of energy that is no longer but a memory in my body, but that, in the old dilapidated body, there is no longer the least possibility of suggestion. When one cannot one cannot. Now Ève cannot die. There

Préparation — Cours N° 5

la phase de dilatation et d'expulsion

Les phénomènes normaux dilat.
Phase d'expuls.
répond n'dat. organisme sollicit pas
besoins et adaptat chac.ponds.
préparat antérieures de l'A.
1 Contract uté. peu f L
on fait de contract. aucun de
pression a l'interi. de l'U. — Rétablis
bb poussée vers col, et col attiré
vers le haut.

Un amincissemt de la parti. infér. U.
La fête de bb en contract. plus
intense avec le col.
Renouvellemt de l'rythm. av vage.
pland. pério. par ou bb passe
Anyrai de l'élasticité fibrous.
Act : à quelle date? B.D. P. super.
valeur théorique, valable 10 jrs
parés. Ocart contract. le tout de
l'iuteriorité.
Au : mod f. contract. de l'A.
réguliers. espacées. rhythme penot.
2 h. 1/4 les 5' Angle. d'incluent.
L' Orifice intern. dilat, tête presser
bas, col attiré en haut.
Bruite l'intensité du col l'iu-
corporé dans le corps. col effacé.
Dilatation.
Il y a les phénom nerveux qui
vont au cerveau ; au début f.
mouvements bb.
Au la contract. plus sensibles.
on sent l'appuie de bb sur col.
Membranes Mallor de bandrech.

Confit d'Artichaut

enlever feuilles et perles
étranger + sau. Hy de l'Eau froid
faire 2 min de Sauté et cuire

Sauté Poireaux père + sel

250 gr. chèvre frais - olives noires marjolaine
épinards + Ayuglecture + huile de coconut
et orange balsamique
crème liquide

Grèce

Mon univers - Confon la Vénitienne
Relieques sept. Auguri (rampa majeur garçon)
Vichy de Flavre La Règle d'Or
Je gula jardins + Flavre
Museums Rodfort Pantlames
viewarks la Sumer ever

has to be someone for that. No image of herself. Her soul stretched out behind the pile of bandages wonders what state her box is in.

How can one live what is not life, don't know how to do that, says my mother to herself. Living she knows. But the other? What doesn't happen to happen, what drags her like dirty rags.

Will it live? my baby is little, it looks old and willing. I change it. I show the Brazilian male nurse how to do it. It is not the first time. I undo its nappy. Where are the clean nappies? Naturally nothing is ready. I find a nappy that is too small so I patch it up. My baby goes along with it. It doesn't open its eyes. It is a few weeks old. When leaning over it I see loads of little pale and thick hairs around its lips. That amuses me. It really is not pretty. I say to myself that perhaps the day when it opens its eyes and looks at us a beauty will come to it of which for the moment it is deprived. For it is the gaze that delights.

–I don't understand this dilapidation, I say. –It is not life, my daughter thinks. It is life that is not in life, thinks my daughter, thinks and does not say it to me. –I don't understand, I say while wringing my hands. She doesn't know how to do anything but live, I say. –You are thinking more slowly than your thought, thinks my daughter. I am in front of you and I'm waiting for you. –I don't understand, I look behind and not in front, I say, I don't want to understand, it is too painful. –She cannot live any longer, there is nothing to live thinks my daughter. –Ève, I say. Alas I no longer address her. I speak about her. –She hears, says my daughter, but elsewhere, otherwise. –Maman died that beautiful, tender and comical night of 2012. Then she wanted to stay. –Maybe she was afraid of losing you, says my daughter. –She was afraid that I would lose her. Now she is falling apart in front of me. –For a long time she has not been able to think in front of you, thinks my daughter. She is on hold. I find that unbearable, but I don't say so. Not telling you what I think and letting you sift the last grain of sorrow, that's what I can do for you. She will never again say to you 'y'reright'. Thinks my daughter.

In reality Ève should have stopped her march on 15 April, thinks Victoire, but Ève is extranatural one absolutely cannot foresee what she is going to invent, on the one hand because she has powers that medicine cannot account for, on the other hand because the soul has its secret wills, which even escape the will of the subject. In the case of Ève, there is in her a being that is mixed with the flour of Hélène. The being secreted in Ève is not governed by the common human fate but by the force of attraction of the absolute. Ever since Ève reached in reality the boundaries of common life, she slipped for better or worse between the bars into an ill-known life that escapes observation and speculation, for it takes form day after day (although there is no 'day' in this 'life') in order to respond, in response to the *vision* of the absolute, in other words of the love beyond love. One can neither neglect nor take into account the invisible and extrabiological factors that entirely modify and exceed the facts verifiable by experience and produce realities of another kind, and that can remain only in the absolute, thanks to the energy of the ideal. Victoire follows this story with the extramedical passion of a true reader, thus overtaken page after page by the woman explorer whose Life is written beyond the lives of the persons that have been reported by literature. The particular feature of this story is that it seems very likely that all of the actors ignore that they have passed the boundaries of the known and the probable and that they are going forward, after passing the medical limit, blindly, and like travellers transported without feeling it from one continent to another, with the minimum of baggage, without goal, without money, sometimes in invisible planes. The various women travellers go forward while tottering in a magical blindness. No one ventures to take 'measures', since everyone feels embarked upon *The Improbable*, a funny sort of minimum boat

–I take as a principle an absolute trust in Victoire, I say to my daughter. –I trust Ève's hidden will. Says Victoire. This will is hidden in the hidden will of Hélène. –I don't know if Maman wants what my mother always wanted, Hélène thinks, tell me, I say to Ève, and I will do it. But I don't know if I am addressing the goddess with shining eyes who would pluck me out of nothingness or the old baby that my mother left in my keeping when she went on board *The Improbable* hanging onto the arm of her cane, how long ago was it?
–In 2006, says my daughter who forgets nothing. After her first pneumonia. Another than herself came out of death, I remember. We were at the hospital without angels.
–I have forgotten

–She is going beyond her strength, says my daughter. –She has gone beyond her strength. You have gone beyond your strength and she as well. She has gone beyond your strength, says my son. These words light up as little candles. Are extinguished. One moment I saw or thought I saw through my shadows. It was but webs of anxieties, I saw enormous spiders running away and I did not kill them.

Shame or not, one doesn't kill, she is being killed, slowly, otherwise other, shame or not one doesn't kill one lets a baby who was born old sink into the malignant mud of Nothingness. I love her viscerally I tremble I kiss her I betray her. Or not? She has passed the gate, she doesn't hear me, I don't hear her. There where she is, desire, will, all the emotions that *make* the future are like her skin, burned, devoured.

An explosion in me: the fire has reached my brain. A voice of fire leaps out of me. I call Victoire. My voice of fire says: 'Enough.' I note that she is strangely cold. Victoire says: 'Lamaline.' The voice says: 'I am climbing through error.' Victoire says: 'Lamaline.'

I have never heard such an ambiguous, malicious name, I say to my daughter. –Who is it? –The archangel of extremity, I say. Lamaline! It's remedy itself, a remedy that poetises our anguish. I think of you, Baudelaire.

I lie down with the cats at my mother's feet. The day dawns, gleams, my mother is sleeping profoundly for Lamaline poured her a magical soporific. My rage as well, put to sleep with Lamaline.

What are we doing? We continue, blindly, skipping from fear to fright. Fear of being awakened afterwards attached to a sin, a fault, an error, of having the light cut off and of being shut up for eternity in the labyrinth of guilts, fear of living or of having lived or of not having lived or of not living the surplus hour or day or of having missed hearing rightly the last word, fear of translating the silence fear of not translating it fear of not and fear of having had backwards courage. I am lacking everything. She does not suffer from suffering, she groans from a painless and unknown suffering. Ève evades. Rolled in a ball. Lets herself slide. Interminable Lethe. No life but death is far. Far? Fear of not knowing how to translate 'far'.

She becomes a poor mole without claws, who doesn't know how to burrow. Only her hands move, but all by themselves, without her arms, without direction. Her hands no longer grasp no longer hold. You could hold the glass with your right hand, I say, but then what to do with a glass that she can't bring to her mouth? And there is no more mouth. So she folds her paws on her breast and looks like a squirrel killed in a fall. She makes her body the coffin.

I am suffering from this endless end, it's the end I say to myself on 20 July, I am suffering from the lost end, I am suffering from the continual end, I lost it, which causes me a double suffering because I lost it at the end, I don't know where when, in Mayjune or long before, in the end

I didn't know where she was exactly, I was afraid of losing the end, it seemed to me that our life, so long and so joyful, risked rotting at the last moment, 'in the space of a minute' as in the case of Mr Valdemar, of being annihilated, our election denied, our unbreakable alliance broken like a glass ring, we were descending, with that violent slowness that makes unhappy people feel each centimetre of degradation, I was groping. As I couldn't hold her hand since she suffered from the least emphatic contact, by her side I would hold in my hand a virtual hand of Maman, I would look at her hand streaked with browning purples from the haematomas and with its well-trimmed, colourless nails. She held her hands on her chest while sleeping, in the end she was holding herself, if there could exist a jealousy of a beloved person who gives herself her hand and repels ours, I would have felt it. I was famished from a famine other than the one that was really famishing her, since she no longer wanted to eat, she turned her tongue against herself, I on the contrary was hungry for every crumb of her, and the crumbs are so rare, or the glory of a gaze, oh! all that a gaze can lavish while transfusing life itself in a second, and more than life, the authorisation to be but she would no longer advance a gaze from between her eyelids except very rarely, and this super-brief and unforeseeable gaze would not greet the face that was begging, a door was not opening, it was the rapid glance of one besieged.

If I didn't have the notebook to reassure myself that she looked at me more than once and the last time on the last day I would feel exiled

I note down nothing. Toneless weeks of an immobilised June in the ice of a meantime, I abandon myself, I let me be a self who mimes Ève, inert and quasi aphasic in her iron cradle.

I had dreamed of a celebration. In the dream we would have stood side by side, with interlaced hands, she would have raised toward me her old confident face, asking me gently with her gaze placed in my eyes: where we going, my great darling? I would have lowered my eyes to her and I would have said while smiling at her perpetually, to the garden of the last act, there will be four-coloured geraniums and magnolias, and behind us one can make out the rose-coloured foot of the Strasbourg cathedral, we are posing bathed in a peaceful aura, Maman is not afraid, without taking her eyes off me, her long nose raised toward my nose that overhangs her, she says thátsgood, while strongly accenting the first syllable, which makes the word sound like an ámen, then the dream transports us offstage and I see us from behind, me on the right of the dream, taller by a head than Ève wrapped up in her white parka and a little lop-sided leaning on her cane that she holds firmly with her left hand.

I wanted it to be a celebration. Instead of that this treacherous dance: one wants it, one throws oneself furiously toward it and it sends us off to its twin, life in shreds. And when one adjusts it tears away from us one shred after the other

Ève was cadenced march. Stretched out in this rigid June, turned over and 'fed', that is forced beyond her forces, enclosed between the large bars, disinterested. That she once opens her eyes is the event of 14 June. We thought that she would not open them again. Thus she is making her way with eyes closed, her mouth hermetic. Her face pink, regular, her mouth is going, is no longer, her nose is growing larger. A maze of wrinkles bristling with hairs below her nose, a chin that expands. Some energy in her head that she can shake feebly. That's less tiring than to go looking for a yes or a no at the very bottom of the well. What strength one has to muster to swallow. Throat exhausted. With a shattering astonishment one observes mammalian life run aground, a giant who goes on working up to the last second. Thus one lives even *after*.

Ève who in my memory had always simplified my life, I say to my daughter on 26 July 2013, removed obstacles with a determined hand, who had cut the knots the way she trimmed the large bass in the kitchen, while congratulating herself on her wise choice and her mind that never wasted time, my mother who neatly sorted out three of my misfortunes, and even more than once paid a ransom so as to allow me to retrieve my freedom, which I had carelessly mortgaged, as rapidly as possible, she who, a modest and lucid general, knew how to decide upon the strategies that were the most economical in human life, she who didn't take two days to leave Germany at the *first* speeches of Hitler, and who took the *first* plane Algiers–France in 1972 as soon as the police cast an invitation her way, she who always took the shortest route, who did not do five round-trips from the table to the kitchen, but cleared everything away *in one go* with her wheeled cart, going five times faster then the average individual about her affairs – it is now she, the strong one, the faithful one, who was dragging me into the labyrinths of calculations, contradictions, about-turns, into the errors of reason, I was lending her thoughts that I was borrowing from her, I doubted that of which I was convinced, the truth is I didn't know any longer if Ève was in my mother, but this truth was totally hidden from me. I would have needed my relief mother to help me to help Maman and thus me. No doubt if she had been conscious, if she had borne herself upright at my side as she had always done, if she had seen me doubled up with anguish by the side of a Medicalisedbed, she would have cut the knots and without blinking and without telling me. But the Relief was bedded down on a plate, its fins cut off, its eyes lacklustre. I considered this blow from fate with dread. I had always known that nothing would stop the spontaneous impulse of her bias. She loved me. And here she was herself the cause of my troubles and lost relief. She could do nothing for me. Worse yet not being able to do anything for her that I was certain was good, I was suffering from a double powerlessness, mine doubled hers. But the most awful thing was since I was suffocating, paralysed with various kinds of powerlessness that were causing each other, I sometimes had the hallucinatory sensation that we were drowning together and in this drowning we were fighting with each other in opposite directions to deliver us mutually from an adverse embrace. As I have already said, when she would say no it was also a yes. –Do you want to drink? –No. And she would drink. And I was wondering if she drank against herself and for me or if she drank against the grain. She wanted me to want for her on my behalf or on her behalf, while she was sleeping.

She has moved into a deep, padded sleep, from which she does not exit, windows closed, eyes closed, the door is padlocked I tap with my index finger on her chin, I slip the end of the little spoon along the thin junction line of what were lips –Open! I say. –Your mouth! says Roro. –Soup! I say. –A tiny spoonful! I say. Doesn't answer. You would do that, says the notebook, I noted everything down, page 18, 18 June 2013 a Tuesday, so now there is between us a door that doesn't open. I remind you, says the notebook, I am there for that. One month, two months, and already the doors are closing, ask Hamlet, 1 August is like ten years from 18 June. Without me, you couldn't believe for a moment that you had made such a cruel journey. Without his ship's log, Shackleton would have kept from his horrifying Antarctic odyssey only the coagulated submemory in a single frozen image of a moment melted in a white abyss. I cannot even say that I have forgotten, I say to my daughter. (On 11 August. We are sitting on Ève's bed in her room in Arcachon.) Is forgetting the name of this furnace that devours my heart, and in the middle of which I weep?

You gave to me, you took back from me. You gave me to think to taste the acrid taste of the life of humans. We have entered into the *Wasteland*, Maman, on 14 June. We are going down the river almost motionless while going nowhere. I decide to bring you to Arcachon. In a large Mercedes Vivo, to go down towards the sea asleep wake up beneath the oak trees or don't wake up continue to dream that you are going down in the Mercedes Vivo boat with me by your side straight like a large tired-out fish that entrusts itself to the current. I will carry you off during your sleep, my old nymph, I will follow my desire not to be separated from you who is myself by the fear of death that is already death itself. Let us flee together, my old Galatea, carried off motionless. Ah! flight takes hold of me, myself by fleeing I flee from myself and I fear fleeing from you. Woe to me, the round of fears makes me dizzy. Error has become my tenant. It touches upon all my desires with the tips of its fingers and instantly they turn into their opposites.

'Can I flee with Ève to the garden down there?' I ask Victoire. It's a folly that one must do, thinks Victoire. No one can say whether the garden is paradise or hell. If I don't take her flight, I kill her, I say to myself.

–She had good sense, says my daughter. –You think I took the wrong direction, I say while wringing my hands. 1 August I do not sleep the whole night I see the enormous black Mercedes Vivo heading toward us. –She was not someone who projected, says my daughter. She followed her own direction. Until 2011 she knew what she did not want.

We will go to Arcachon, I say to myself, in her sense. She said the word *Arcachon* on 22 May. On 1 June everything is ready for the descent to paradise. It's a challenge. The passive traveller is laid down in the big shiny black car by shoving her like unleavened bread into the rolling oven and we leave precipitously by the grace of God. We will make the trip as usual, I say to myself, with one difference: my mother will be stretched out on a triple seat, the catheter bag turned toward me. A cortege of fears will not leave us.

But between 23 May and 1 June Ève had become another and I was thinking in opposites and obstinates.

Deep down in my imagination that was ceaselessly projecting scenarios, catastrophes for the most part, silhouettes kept passing from *As I Lay Dying* or the *Odyssey*: journeys that don't progress.

–I will accompany you, says my son. I myself would not go *under any circumstances*, says my son. But in spite of myself and for you I will do what I myself would not do in any circumstance. I find this trip completely mad. I am descending with you into madness. I don't hesitate to tell you this on this afternoon of Thursday, 27 June 2013. –Why wouldn't you do it? I say –Because I would be afraid, says my son. I'm not afraid to tell you that.

I lose sight of myself every day, I write on 18 June, I am wandering, I am not who I was yesterday, I am steering myself with the notebook, the paper can be trusted, not me. Don't forget, says the notebook: two days ago, she said: 'some milk'. I say: 'hot or cold?' She says: 'cold'. Never before has she asked for milk. In her whole life. I thought it was ten days ago. It was then 16 June, says the notebook, so on 14 June. I noted the milk on the 16th. You are reading me this on 18 June, says the notebook. Already the milk is far away.

'Hélène!'
She called you on 27 June, in the afternoon. That's all I noted that day, says the notebook. This 12 August I still hear the notes of this song, this brief music that I will never lose, it is not a call, whatever the notebook might say, it's a greeting. There is an invisible syllable in the modulation, the note of regret, as if the pain of losing me were exhaling with force the pain of losing me, while getting lost. 'Maman! I exclaimed. My beloved!' That's all we wanted: to knot our voices together.

–She is losing her hair, says the nurse. Mustn't get a bedsore on her head. The idea of an additional wound wounds me. –If that's the way it is I exclaimed, on 20 June, we stop! Enough with these deathly little tasks of the end! But in reality I do not cry out.
I am wrong, I say to my daughter. *I have become doubtful.* Doubt spreads, everywhere its odour of crime rises.

How many dead people I am! The woman of love triumphant whom I lost in February 2005 in the death of my beloved. I was no longer the principal character of a secret epic. My mother was only ninety-five years old, I knew that she loved me regularly, with her planetary movement, without eclipse, without deviation. And now it's the enchanted daughter of Ève from Osnabrück, the cantor of the two Klein sisters who is shown the door of the world of the living.

I doubt in my bones. I fear and flee myself. I am suffering terribly from the hachet and asphyxia. I miss Maman's light, she no longer places her great confident gaze in my eyes. It's decided, we will flee. We will go and hide behind the pines. I doubted. This June is poisoned.

–She doesn't know how to do anything but live, I say. Dying, no, she didn't study it. –She was not there when Omi died, says my daughter. She was at the market. –I am the one who thought that she was no longer in life. Says my daughter. –That's true. I thought that this wasn't life. Think I. –I found that unbearable. Says my daughter. Thought I.

Says the notebook, on 1 August. But it said more or less the same thing on 22 June. And having written in a state of distraction, I didn't know if it was Anne or a me wandering from me to me that June who had thought to say that.

That Ève be removed from this world, I say, it's as if the Fifth Brandenburg Concerto had been stopped, put in a cage, burned, reduced to ashes, its first gay, red, dancing movement, that's her, that's my nymph, what am I saying, Ève taken away for me it's as if one had totally lost Bach, I listen to the flute running through the concerto, that's my mother's burst of laughter, which rises up to her nose, her good humour, her sneezes, her solidity of a tower up until the bombardment of 13 January, she is altogether under the sign of the inexhaustible, I say.

'You want to leave!' thunders the nurse to the sound of cymbals. LEAVE! Bang! Want! The crash of the percussion overturns the silence and smashes into my mother's window. This shot terrorises me. I clutch the right-hand bars of the Medicalisedbed. 'You don't want to eat!' WANT! KLANG! It's Bartók, it's Bluebeard, it's Boris Godunov, I stammer, gripped by convulsions, 'don't shoot!' 'But yes she does, she hears me,' booms the nurse. 'She knows what she wants,' says the nurse who knows what she wants, while I am projected outside myself.

'One doesn't dare to leave,' says the nurse in flowers. 'One is waiting to be alone.' That's what the nurse says. She speaks very loudly. She says: 'You have an extraordinary daughter. She agrees. She permits you to leave.' She cries while articulating very strongly to be sure that however far she is in the *Wasteland* my mother can hear. I am seized by trembling. The words drive their thorns into my throat, I want to vomit the terror. I don't confide this to the notebook. Instead of that I lose my soul, from 3 o'clock in the afternoon until evening. Error and doubt are perched like vultures on my shoulders. *That* I cannot write down, the nurse with the violet eyes leaning like an angel over Maman, me beside the Medicalised bed in a convulsion. *That* I remember. I found that unbearable. This kind of truth with violet eyes.

–Your daughter permits you to leave! She agrees. –Don't say that, I yell. And no sound came out of the shadow of my mouth and I remained sunk in horror for several hours and I couldn't speak to anyone, and I say nothing to the notebook. The nurse with the springtime eyes was translating my mother into French, she thundered, she spelled out: 'leave! until tomorrow!' Don't say, I wanted to say, 'I say what she wants, thundered the angel with trumpet, she hears me, I tell you.' Then Ève's empty mouth opens and a low and clear croaking pronounces slowly: 'until tomorrow'. I remain sunk in Lethe until evening.

When I manage to come out of the river with its excessively salty viscous waves, I find myself lying on my son's chest, and I remember nothing. According to the notebook, this scene would have taken place in reality and at the very end of the month of June.

A mistake that I don't recognise as mine is misleading me, I make mistakes by proxy, I am inside, the mistake is the air I breathe. These blanks, these silences in the notebook, sometimes I ran away from it the way I was running away from myself or my dreams. Then I was filled with despair once more, and once again the notebook wept. I believe I wondered once who this very patient, very hospitable note-book was to whom I could speak. And if this thin notebook of sixty pages would suffice to accompany me until the end of this 2013 life, the slowest, the most agitated and all the same the most stagnant year I have ever lived.

Today, 14 August, it becomes obvious to me that the notebook could only be Maman. No doubt during these blanks she was asifdead and thus me too. Or else on the dock of the Lethe, motionless, timeless. Nothing was happening, neither life nor death. We must have taken refuge hanging from a rocky overhang.

Galatea (for my misfortune) throws me an apple, says Kepler, says my son, and runs away. *Malo me Galatea petit, et fugit ad salices*, she throws me an apple, says Virgil, says Kepler, launches my son at me, and it's the dance of Error, that is the fate that Ève throws to us, she throws us a mischievous apple, and in the same moment she flees, toward the willows, she calls us and doesn't respond to us, you want it? what do you want? I'm coming! nothing! she laughs and she flees to hide herself I believe I'm mistaken, like her, where are we going? *ad salices*, as far as the willows, but I don't like weeping willows, says my mother, they look sad. But before hiding, remarks Virgil, the cunning Galatea, error in person, *se cupit ante videri*, she wants, says Kepler, to have been seen, and that is why you are suffering, says my son from the awful ambiguous charms of error, Ève wants you to want and does not want to want, she is in her bed as in the willows, as in a foreign land. Woe is me, Galatea leaves me only to come back to flee, she mocks my vertigos, when I think she is calling me she repels me. –You said to me: come, I say. −Me? I said nothing to you, says Galatea, I threw you an apple. I said nothing.

The apple, I say, is doubt itself, is it the good fruit is it a misunderstanding? I thought you had said: fruit. Me? I said: scoot.

Galatea, the error spiders the Medicalisedbed. I am going backward, I am in perpetual cancellation. My hearing is bewitched. The apple hits me in the ear. *Malo me! Malo me!* I don't know any longer in which language I hear the language of Maman who flees while throwing sibylline sayings at me: 'Goobye! T'late! 'Thing!'

'I'm not afraid,' says Ariane in a voice that in fact does not tremble, is not afraid, takes a step that's merely a step, whereas I take ten opposite steps to take one half-step and as soon as I stand up I sit down.

In my dream of 20 to 21 June 2013 the sea rises everywhere and inundates all the way up to the eyebrows of my large house. Thus I will weep for my house. This morning, everything is golden and in flower, Ariane is not afraid and I tremble between the words.

The word life, I say. For example, life, life, life, one lives life. Rhymes with strife, says my mother. I don't know any longer, did I ever know it, where life begins to veer off despite life, am I living?

Ariane says farewell to her house that is all light and in traces of planets. No apple-flight, Ariane *seizes* the initiative and she cuts. An absence of hesitation is her internal goddess.

Life without pleasure, life without glimmer. There is no reference any longer, I say. Needy life, grandiose tenacity. Galatea phones me from the willows and says: I will always betray you my dear.

Ariane leaves her house before she leaves it. My house is collapsing slowly on my head, the inundation carts off letters, books, beds, bandages.

–When the sea was rising in her house, Éri called Ève, and she said to her: 'j'en ai marre', in French, I say. So Ève says to her sister: 'if you've had enough, well then you can leave'. They said *au revoir* to each other in French, I say – their foreign language. Not in German or in English. Ève had an absence of hesitation.

–Until she was confined to bed says Anne, Ève enjoyed life, and life was the synonym of enjoyment.

–Madame C. has the air of someone who doesn't realise, said the Hospital.

–Is air another synonym of life? I am airless, I say to myself. Flee, says my mother, without r. Éri said: Ève, *j'en ai marre*. They had learned this word *marre* upon arriving in Paris as young girls from Osnabrück, which they left without any hesitation.

It's difficult for me to recopy these pages from the notebook: the notes confuse several periods and several houses. I never knew in which house I was, in which end, in which life.

–I didn't note down the day when Ève had enough, *marre*, I say to Ariane. I suffer from having missed the telephone call.

–You don't deserve this, says Ariane. –One always gets what one doesn't deserve, I say. –I am ready, says Ariane. –She has not said *j'en ai marre* in French, I say. But perhaps in another language. And it would have escaped me? But how?

But here Ariane cuts the rope I wind around my neck. And says: ....

(I am content to write these pages in French without any detour. I have been thinking about it since 3 July. I reach the summit on 15 August 2013. On 15 August 1960 was born by Ève's hands my distressed son, the commander of my first shipwreck, and it was the same hands of Ève Cixous midwife that opened in September 1961 to let the simpleton child depart. Everything is coincidence. Ève was never afraid, the word *life* was as natural to her as the sun)

Then Ariane says (and I'm not afraid to say today what traversed the house like a meteor on 21 June): 'I am ready to make the move. I am not afraid to say it out loud. I promise. If you want I will be in the bedroom tomorrow. I propose to you to give, I propose to you to stop. I say and I do.'

She talks for a long time

I listen.

She plays a big word that roars like a cannon shot, on purpose to prove to me that she is afraid of nothing, she got her courage from Aeschylus, it is a raw courage, worthy of the innocent crimes of the gods. What word? The notebook tells me: the word 'accomplice'. In case you are doubtful, I am witness, says the notebook. She laid down the word of Athena twice, notes the notebook. Otherwise I would have thought I dreamt it. Saying the word in a loud voice, she goes crimson. I contemplate her person with admiration. 'Go without fear. I will return with you and I will do what is right,' says the goddess. She put on her angry eyes, with their irises of transparent gold. Beneath her voice everything is clear. From my shadow I raise my ears toward the Milky Way. How frontally one thinks up there! as for me I listen in profile.

I cannot say yes. This cannot is extended over me like a black cloud full of voices.

I listen to it.

It says: '... the angels of Osnabrück'. It says: 'tranquillisers'. The voices whistle, bellow. I hear teeth clacking, jaws trembling. Maman's rusty voice wanders, Hélène! A very small pallid character, very long, skinny, hollow cheeks, that's me. Says: 'We will see after the summer.' You said that, says the notebook.

It says: –I remember that you confided to me that she herself had (*whereupon enters*: the ghost of my dying son carried in my mother's strong hands, his head falls back on the side) ... –It's true, I say. She has always had tender courage, heroism without heroism, unconditional love.

From the cloud the voices bleat, a flock of hoarse angels. You fear, you fear? Still Galatea? Fear of the bad mistake. Fear of cowardice. Fear of betraying her trust. But I am betraying her trust. Help me! What do you want? Nothing. Don't you hear then? I told you: Nothing. What are you waiting for?

–The end of summer.

–Take anything you want, says Ariane. Lamps, cushions, armchairs, beds, books.

–I want the walls on which the beloved dead wrote their names.

I want to know what to do so that my mother continues to love me after the summer, to wait for me, without worrying, so as to enjoy the ambrosia of fidelity.

My admiration for Ariane makes me dizzy. She keeps neither objects nor traces. One is shipwrecked, one gets back up again. Neither this temple-house, full of letters from all the peoples of the world, of memories of wars and resurrection, of furniture that comes from the flowers of evil, of beds full of the odours of melancholias. Without regret.

Exactly the opposite of me. Feverish sanctuary that I am. I gather up the fur of the cats between my pages. The hairs of my beloved in my address books. She throws away, ends, leaves, takes the air. And yet, she keeps. But where? Crouching under the cloud, I listen to her, there flutters above my head fear and recognition, I sink beneath the powdery black earth.

–You gave me something unique, I say, you put a sharp gaze in my misty eyes.

–What have you eaten? says Ariane.

–I don't want what I want, I say. No, that's not it. I want what I don't want.

–Eat a good rare piece of meat. And some foie gras. Honour the work of all those little producers who struggle lovingly. And also some oysters.

–I am haunted by the filial sentiments of a parricide, I say.

–Come back down to this good earth, says Ariane. Thin is okay, skinny is not.

–You're the one saying that? Right away I thought that I was my mother. Those were her words, I heard her voice behind your voice.

–What your mother did for your son, with her typical absence of hesitation, I will do, I'm not afraid, says Ariane armed with her sovereign absence of hesitation. That's what life is. I will go with you. One has to know how to cut, says my mother. When it's time it's time.

I vacillate. Now, I say to myself, it is Ève who is in the place of my son, and Ariane is in the place of my mother, thus in my place, since my mother put herself in my place.

–Do you want the large Chinese bowls? There are ten of them.

–We will make soup for the angels, I thought. It occurred to me that, in order to interrupt my mortal oscillation, I need the help of the being-altogether-other-than-me, capable of the *effective action* shown by Giotto's angels in the eyes of Marcel. Those who *do not fail* to flutter around in front of the stumbling saints.

    –It's necessary to cut, says Ariane with her beautiful sculptor's hands. Before me flutters 22 June.

You thought of her hands, the notebook reminds me. All that she did with her hands (cutting, pruning, piercing, sewing, bringing out the head, repairing, severing, dismantling, hammering). All her strength in her well-made hands. It's in her fingers that her determination resides. I see her finishing her glass of red wine and banging it down on the table, boom! afterwards. *Fertig!* I jumped. A brief, surprising violence. As if there were a man within her thin silhouette. Perhaps her father? An authority.

    What remains of it: the clarity of her utterances: No! Yes! Enough.

Ève is keeping watch. This morning, 22 June 2013, for an instant she opened her eyes wide, which she had not done in weeks. 'I live,' said her eyes. Then she left again. I didn't have time to talk to her.

23 June 2013. Anne agrees with Ariane. Says: –I can give. Says –Finally you have clarity, you said the sentence. –What sentence? I say. –The one you said, says Anne. –What did I say? I say. –It is necessary to let her leave. –That sentence has left again, I say. I didn't have time. Hesitations chirp deafeningly around my lines: am I deaf? am I afraid? did I miss the boat? it left without us.

    Anne takes the side of the sentence. She is going to carry it to Victoire. Ève is sleeping. Lamb, what did I do? What didn't I do? One of the ten angels dived right beside me. Around me silences that are friendly with my silence begin to murmur tenderly. My son agrees with Ariane. 'Your daughter agrees,' says the nurse. I don't agree with myself, at any moment. Pierre-François says: –I will do it. *H.* –For whom? For Ève or for me? Pierre-François says: For you. I will do it for you. I look at my son with admiration. No sooner said than done. It is the first time that I *see* the last scene of a play a long time before the end. Usually I don't know it. The actors bear their destinies without knowing the end. The end arrives like a surprise. It is not at all what I would have imagined. –We will do it together. The end, says my son. –Very well, I say. There, we have a good death.

I cannot forgive myself for something, but I don't know what, it is already 14 July 2013, and I am suffering as if it were the afternoon of 1

July, I am in the pyre, I think it is interminable, a disastrous, inevitable sensation, even if I 'know' abstractly that 'all this is going to pass very quickly', as Ariane says to me on 28 June. –That's what Freud says, says my daughter, one feels guilty, fortunately *she cannot imagine* the horrible pain that this sensation causes, one will give anything in order to die, but in vain, for *in truth one is dead.*

I condemn myself, on 23 June. Today I committed suicide, I say to my son. I ran myself over in a Mercedes Vivo. I reversed myself with my internal opposite who was perhaps me or someone other than me. I was Kafka's killer. I ran away with my mother without knowing if I was saving our life or our death, I no longer remember what I desired, decided, my daughter, it seems to me, tells me Victoire thinks that my flight is madness, it seem to me that Victoire thinks that my flight is madness, it seems to me that Victoire thinks that I must flee but perhaps she thinks that I must flee flight, what do you think I ask my son, my son finds that the flight to Arcachon is total madness, he is ready, Victoire is ready, who said that Ève will escape, the trip is easy, flight is difficult, I no longer know who said what, it's me, says my son, why, I say, because I would be afraid, says my son, I say that wherever it is flight awaits me, we speak with half-words, slips of the tongue, misunderstandings, it's not the flight that is difficult, it's what follows. She permits you to leave, says Violette. I have fallen into horror and I remain under water for several hours with Maman, I say. She's right, says my son. It's necessary for her to know that you let her leave. *Know.* The word *know* strikes me and flees behind Ève's silences. I no longer know who is right who is mad. I am, says Victoire. Ève is driving my madness. Disconnect the battery, says my mother. I will do it, says my son. Put the cards on the table, says my daughter. You want a pill, I say. Leave, says Violette. Come, I say to Ève.

Far, says Ève. Perhaps one doesn't wake up, thinks my mother.

Now we stop Ève's life. Now I withdraw her from my body. Now I look at her. For a long time. Now I weep. Maman runs down my cheeks. I feed her with my tears. She is alive. Now we smile at her. She is sleeping deeply warm and calm. She rests me. Now no more now. Perhaps one is sleeping perhaps one is weeping I thought.

–Where is the peace of the soul? says my daughter –I thought it was in Ève's armoire in Arcachon. There is childbirth without pain in the drawer. –To go down, says my daughter, doesn't it mean to go back up? –The idea of going down back up makes me dizzy.

Ève wants. Ève? *Uralt* Ève in the bed from hell, I say. Now I want to lie down with her and take her in my arms as when I was little, taking her she took me. But I cannot, one cannot touch her, Ève cannot. Like the shade of Anticlea, the mother of Ulysses. One can no longer touch her. When? I say. When never, says Victoire. The idea that I could embrace her alive only by killing her, I cannot let it touch me, I flee. Nothing that causes suffering, says Victoire, to stop, everything that causes suffering, Ève is going to decide. Ève does not want. To eat, to move, to touch, to want. Respect this indifference, says Victoire. *I want to sleep.* She is not going to be able to stay for long, says Victoire. Do not force her to. Y'reright, says my mother. We're going to vote in the European elections, I say. –Where is my card? says my mother. –In your pocket. She could stay for a few months, says Violette. How long does a long time last, I ask my son. Sunday tears me to pieces still on Monday. I no longer know the name of the day, yesterday, where the word *stay* came to be thrown like an apple into my hands, I wanted to take Maman into my arms but she has withdrawn behind the sheet. Let sleeping take the controls, says Victoire.

How Maman grows and fills my whole body and soul and overflows from my eyes. She is my treasure, my beloved nymph. She would raise her old nose toward me in order to know, from my eyes, what I wanted her to want. Stopping has re-entered the house. One cannot imagine anyone more alive than Maman.

What does one call that, not enough strength to come back up and live not enough strength to die? I say. She floats in her lukewarm boat, breathes regularly, dreams, in this metamorphosis I am transformed into columns of tears, I carry her body without touching it.

I see them in the Samuel Beckett avenue, all the shades of Memory that are preparing to enter into my being. I hate them but it is perhaps love. All the buildings and the trees crowd toward me, I see us already on the bench in front of the house, sitting all three of us, Roro, Ève and me for an eternity begun in March 2012. I enter into Hades by the bench.

The turnaround-decision to Let her Sleep having struck me like a thunderbolt, it's as if while leaning over the balcony I had let her fall on the bench. In any case it's on Ève's bench that I find the notebook again. Under the shock, all the days that crowd around our boat like the trees of the avenue seem to form but one day, which I lose, which repeats itself, which I repeat, in a maelstrom of times that comes back to sit, dream, stand up, fall from the balcony.

I could hold her back. Keep her sleeping in her boat wandering on the surface of outside-time, if I were her boat. I follow her boat with my eyes. My children stand up and call me in a strong voice, delicately. I sleep. I hear them. Their firm, gentle voices. I understand that they have left silence behind once and for all. They will not be quiet.

Ève is silent. Does not come back: stays, stays herself. Charming sweet, obedient. 'Do you want a drink?' She seeks for long time in the depths of her body a drop of response, finds, opines lightly. I introduce a spoonful of water, her mouth reflects. Slowly. Applying itself. 'Do you want a little compote?' She nods her head distantly. But her lips remain closed in front of the spoon. I could shake her. Tap her cheeks, her chin. It is 25 June, or perhaps 27 June. I stay in front of her lips.

–You tried at 9 o'clock, noon, 1 o'clock, 3 o'clock, says the notebook. Do you want a drink? She: slight yes of the head, but the mouth resolute, closed. –And at 5 o'clock? I asked. Not noted, says the notebook. You listened. To the right the tick-tock of the clock. To the left breathing as regular as the clock. At 7 o'clock in the evening she turns her head toward her right. Partly opens her eyes by a millimetre. Raises the covers a little. Scratches a little around her eye. Noticed me. Goes back to sleep.

Not noted the thoughts of the subject hanging on the bars. Only the word: Nothing.

What a road we're on! Slowly descending slow descent, wherewegoing, to Arcachon it rhymes with Acheron thinks my mother, perfect, tender, giant, smouldering under the ashes. Hearing her breathe gives me life. One could live like this: breathing.

We have reached the threshold of poverty. How rich we were yesterday. Our voyages roll out rivers of images between the banks of my soul, between the bars of the Medicalisedbed, all our Germanys, and our Chicagos, then the tower of the Montsouris park. From year to year it shrinks, then we are sitting in the armchair in the living room, then we are folded in the iron bed, then we don't get up any more. Then I abstain from washing her, a useless torment. Then we grant ourselves peace. We are in the last train. The bed grumbles. Between us the bars.

A sand storm comes up and sweeps away the days in a great death rattle. Whoosh! Oblivion drops its sheet of sand in one fell swoop over the weeks, the months perhaps. It's, I say to myself, that I *cannot keep* the memories of the states that are both violent and totally opposite of the me's that jostle each other in me around my mother overturn each other, cancel each other, deny each other, argue with each other within my walls, put me out of tune with myself to the point of madness. I anger *myself*. I offend *myself*. I scold, growl at myself against myself, I scratch my nose. I want to die alive, thinks my mother, I want to scratch my nose, at the last minute, scratch my head, don't claw, scratch. I scratch my mother's head. You're not going to make me totter at the edge of the abyss, I think. It is *dif*-fi-cult, thinks my mother. –What is difficult? –To be living and dying at the same time. –I had never thought of that, I say, semi-living semi-Maman semi-buried beneath the sand. How fearful and lacking imagination we are, poor deicide mortals, refuges of false ideas, hostages of illusions of innocence and guilt. I cling to my mother's hair, I hang onto her fingernails.

I note that on the 25th you were thrashed by a terror of bottomless loss, which left you on the floor. This 25th was disproportionate, disoriented. P.-F. said: –I am coming to sleep at your house. This sentence casts me into a mad anxiety. –We are still alive! I cried, on 25 June. One has to reach the beyond, the unexplored zone where blow all kinds of suffering, we are still far from that, I cried. Where is the beyond? I would say. My cheek was on my son's breast, a maternal pillow. –Nothing is lost, sings my pillow-son. I will make a Homeric list of everything that Ève is leaving me, I will compose Ève's shield, not one scene will be missing, not one bit of string, not one rubber band cut from a pink rubber glove. She has given. One has received. Now I give you a lesson on the frontier and the border. While P.-F. sings melodiously, my mind goes off with Ève, I am unable to listen to the stanzas. I say: –I'm foolish. My son says: –Finally! He draws and writes '*domain*' and '*frontier*' and '*border*'. Suddenly between the tears I understand where I am lost. I find myself lost. To find oneself lost is the air I breathe with Ève.

Now, I thought, you can depart, my adorable beloved.

Already the house is swarming with embryos of memories. From the refrigerator, the calls of Ève's compote and *café au lait* rise as soon as I open it. –What will I do with the soup? –Eat it, says my son. But I can't find the strange courage to eat my-mother-the-soup. –Throw it away. Neither eating nor throwing away. But neither Solomon nor Abraham comes to give me the response that saves. Finally I decide that I will carry a spoon of my mother in my mouth. Finally I dream that I eat my cats. As I was weeping hot tears yesterday, the two cats curled up by my two sides, with a serious air. Above my head the voice of P.-F. the wind, the breath of mathematical wisdom, '*the frontier cannot be totally diffuse and cannot be a separation*, it says, *the frontier is the set of points that are infinitely close to a thing and a non-thing, is not a delimitation*', it says, here I am transported to the entry of the continent beyond with Maman, via the air, I say to myself, it's a fabulous sensation, we are asleep together and at the same time conscious of being asleep, when I disembark, all the people have already left, I find myself alone, after time, with Ève. '*The frontier between water and air in the fog is not a separation,*' says the prophetic voice, which travels everywhere above my head. '*It is the entire space.*' It soothes me infinitely to recognise that in this way I am with my mother. In the frontier. '*Every point in the fog is at once close to the water and close to the air.*' I am in the fog, with my mother, now I understand, we are the fog. Everywhere stretch Ève's threads, shining silk.

In the *Transnothing Express* with Ève. She has her backpack. She wobbles. She speaks every language, *sprechen sie Deutsch, habla español, do you speak English,* to show that she has all her faculties. The conductor asks: –*What is your name?* –*I forgot.* She lowers her nose. She raises her nose. –*You know it better than me.* She looks at me: she got out of that okay.

And would you believe that the station master who waved his flag was Ariane?

In the fog of the days close to water and air at 9 o'clock in the morning, surprise: she opens her mouth. I quickly pour in water. More. More. She pulls the sheet back up. Wipes her lips. More. Has stocked up for the journey. Then leaves again. Is she going to come back? I slip into the fog with her. We speak silence. At 2 o'clock in the afternoon, I lean down. Her beautiful face. She opens her eyes and says: –Hélène. –I am here. She gives: –Metoo. Or else: 'Iam.' Or else: 'Thank you.' In the fog sounds overflow into each other. I moisten her mouth. We leave again.

Almost not there any more, completely there, there where she is, under, perfectly, metoo, mehere. Me within the outside of my mother, in Ève's fog, neither thick nor thin, I wish passionately to grasp her but she has no border. At 7 o'clock in the evening, I don't know how I find myself outside barred at the iron bars, torn up, leaning over her, drinking in her immaterial mystery, no water, only air, and clearly situated to her right on the side of the armoire, dear Colette and Françoise on the other side slightly leaning as if they were holding themselves back in proximity to the Ève domain. Ève is a little bit everywhere her eyelids perceptibly not closed. One doesn't know what is happening behind the veil: it? wakes, keeps watch, flees, comes? Suddenly she heaves up, sends the rope of her voice very far, calls: –Hélène! H. –I am here! Ève's voice emerges and sets down on the edge of the river very clearly the word: –*Chérie!* –Yes, my love. Miserable happiness to receive the priceless word from the one who no longer has anything. The idea that she does not want to leave without staying with me without turning around while the train takes her away, without weakly waving her hand while time rolls slowly along the dock of the Lethe, that she will never leave me on this earth, that she breaks the silence with vanished strength, that she invents the departure that does not sever, that is all of space, that she finds in the extreme power of her soul the resource, which is unimaginable for science, of the sign beyond the sign, this idea materialises in a flood of tears, I don't know why. All my thoughts pour out, as if they were bursting before they were able to mature.

At 10 o'clock in the evening I pace beside her body, indecisive. She calls: 'Hélène'. I murmur 'Iamhere.' Indecisive a phantom desire takes shape in me, a mythological impulse. If I yelled, if I challenged fate, if I refused the boundaries, if I fought over Ève at the limit of Ève, she would be with me, I have already done that, I have yelled at God more than once, I have fought death over a body, I didn't want to give in and I gave in. Unliveable so much life to die.

I want-her-to-leave-to-rest-herself-to-rest-myself-I-want-to-raise-her-up-bring-her-back-save-myself-with-her-for-her-to-take-me-to-the-Paris-of-dreams, I'm dreaming, right away she arrives, she is going to go and get her suitcase, what a relief she is sixty years old this Ève, and, for a blessed instant, I forget my broken, ground up, exhausted Ève in her iron cage. I come back. I give up wanting what I want. Exhausted, broken I look at Ève immobilised in her remainder of body sending all the strength of her long reign into the battle, but which one

Fog, my only help, be my beacon!

Depart, beloved, depart, while we are still at peace, do not depart, do not depart until Toolate chases us away, depart before Toolate attacks us. Cat-Theia watches me write, I am sitting on the toilet-chair, calm like you. I want to take everyone to the garden in Arcachon.

It is then that the terrible Wednesday erupts. It's a cruel duel, phantomatic is the enemy, the invisible tries to strangle Ève, she fights, from the depths of my miserable sorrow I abandon her I do not help her, my powerlessness does not respond to her, I do not kill her, I do not save her, I lose in a few hours the peace of love of so many years, you are surely right, Montaigne, we mustn't judge our happiness until after death, today I am judging myself, I am separated, before death I am after death, I watch my mother being invaded.

I want absolutely to cry out to Victoire that very evening: 'I am not killing her; I am killing her.' You don't see that I am an assassin. From afar, from my infinite exile, I glimpse Victoire living in a magically colourful world, bathed in golden lights, where real days go by, beings accomplish their tasks there, people ride bicycles, ah! I recognise everything that was my mother, in the past, I have fallen into the cavern of the ego, the walls sweat, a filth glues my thoughts, a dark feeling of dishonour occupies my hold, I feel like a ship whose captain has deserted. 'To die is nothing, it's killing that is the supreme pain' I want to cry out most urgently to Victoire. But my voice bogs down in an internal sand.

I say to my son: –I-don't-do-I-do-grave-things. I am killing myself. –Oh! okay. Yes. But not for long. Says my son.

At an uncertain turning Victoire arrives in my nightmare like the indistinct moment when the dream loses that infinitesimal quantity of its power of enchantment and begins to cede power to the true reality. Lamaline and Xanax, two kinds of Help 'capable' of making a plane take off by suggestion are featured at her sides. Now they enter into our service, alternately, says Victoire, like two servants come from the Castle. For fear of confusing them I inscribe their order of service in the notebook. Since they are foreigners come from Kafka's climate, I welcome them with an interesting mixture of the spirit of eager hospitality and mistrust. I call it misconfidence. It's also because they have names that arouse misconfidence. I sense that Ève appreciates these unintentional jokes. From now on I name for her the medications that bring her their help. She classifies them in the category of 'nice ones'.

(Thursday dawns as if there had been no crime, aggression and betrayal.)

Victoire and I draw up two certificates of life for Ève Cixous née Klein, for Germany. I sign for Ève. All of this in a dream where terror is side by side with salvation.

Ève has never been as calm, as restful as in the following note, a certain day dawns, the storm is erased, terror under opium, my lamb sleeps, smooth, gentle. I am not conscious of the fact that I think I see a lamb when I watch Ève sleep, I think: little child, I don't think: butcher. Yes I would like to sleep with her, hold her in my arms, graze on the grass of dreams, feed on her warmth. But that is what is forbidden to me forever, that is what alreadydead is, my death seated in life without life, that's what alreadysilence is, torture: she is still-there and I cannot touch her. She is here departed. I am thirty centimetres kilometres away from my mother. We are suffering from frontier-tortures, pains, proximities, fingers torn away, crushings of the imagination, for imagination suffers physically.

According to Victoire Ève is not suffering. I don't suspect that for a moment. What tortures me are the torments of her thoughts that wear and tear have weakened and that only cease being agitated by shudders and shivers of fears when she sleeps. When the hurricane swoops down on her dispensing threats of violent death, the only recourse is to hide herself beneath the sheet. I note with chagrin that the sheet is of more help than I.

19 August 2013

One does not at all make literature with this poor suffering. In my study I work for weeks on *As I Lay Dying* with delight. But this has nothing to do with the room where the Medicalisedbed metamorphoses slowly into a coffin. It's chance. Addie Bundren has no relation with Ève. Except that they are strong women. But they are not the only ones. A.B. has no humour. Ève makes rhymes just for laughs with her last breaths.

Under the name of life and with all the attributes of life, death begins to live with us long before its arrival. In this moment I am dying, it is not spectacular, no damage and no one to witness it, but the almost flavourless liquid of the thought of death is spread over everything I taste, it's noticeable in a minuscule separation that slips between my actions and myself, as if a fine membrane got between me and pleasures and good things, an infinitesimal cataract on the heart, on feelings, between my love for others and others. It's the irreversible consequence of having been diminished of my living mother and grafted to my dead mother. I date this state of internal separation from 13 or 14 January but that's a convenience.

One can not know what one knows and believe what one doesn't believe. I am the proof of that. During the whole time Maman was agonising I was also agonising, never did the word agony pierce my thoughts, no doubt it was hiding in the willows with Galatea. But according to my daughter Ève's journey had begun much earlier than I believe, after her first pneumonia, when she was ninety-six, but I don't have the same memory as my daughter, I have totally forgotten the descent from the first floor.

I turned around in the other direction on Friday, 28 June: I am my gay and maternal son, my daughter my friend by half my mother by marvellous inheritance: next stop, Paris. I bring my thoughts and my days back from Arcachon, I slowly get back on the road to Paris. *To stay* in Paris, I was horrified by that until yesterday: as if I remained waiting, while awaiting, the Event. I wanted to die in Paradise. When yesterday my daughter described to me how 'It' would be Hell, the funeral from a distance, the town hall, the police, the law, that is why during the night I left again with my mother in the opposite direction. I dream of a dream in which Arcachon would be in Paris and Ève in the trees with the golden waves and the gods, but the dream does not come.

'AH!' Was that a sigh? It was a noise-thing, an enormous unknown sound. As if someone had brutally entered *into* Ève. In her head. In her field of vision. As if she had been knocked down by a racing car. It was a semi-cry: a cry cut in half. Or as if a shadow had bitten her. It jumped on her back and closed its jaws on her nape. Painless but with stupor. And anger. –Did you hear? That *Ah*? I never heard an *Ah!* so strange, so voluminous, so short, an arrested cry. And this cry-thing pierced my heart. I thought: when Roland's jugular vein burst. *AH!*

This death has a long life. It's as if my mother was the body of Hector interminably dragged by a chariot, and I would be Priam, I beg them to return his body to me because flayed broken ruptured dislocated lukewarm it still palpitates.

With all her strength Ariane pulls me toward the exit. When I say I am staying in Paris in July and for eternity, she is relieved, I narrate town hall police funeral home mortuary, coffin, everything against us, she says what if the police arrest you with a dead body. Thus ends my long dream of freedom travelling with Maman. The administrative jaws snap shut. So be it, let's take the iron plane and leave together for Paris. –I am going to notify the angels of Osnabrück or Oran. Or Strasbourg. They are going to come and get her, says Ariane. –Osnabrück, I say.

Ève is suffering from her luck, I say. I keep her death, thus her repose at a distance, a paradoxical torture. In *Double Oblivion . . .* , Ève says 'I am an old vegetable' 'one must put it in a retirement home'. But then she is a queen. She sleeps gently, just below waking, I don't know at what distance from her body. In dreams she escapes from her old rags.

'I will be in Paris on 25 July,' says Ariane. I am sitting on the stool beside Ève. She is half-sleeping, lets escape a half-gaze, opens a bird's beak, I pour spoonfuls of water for her. This happens on 29 June, Saturday night, my notebook confirms. 'If on 25 July what we are waiting for has not happened, says Ariane, I will be with you. And I will do it.' I sing: my adored beloved, my darling, my old broken bird, are you going to sleep? She nods her head. I am going to tell her, when I have returned to myself, to her, enough travelling, my dear beloved, let's leave together. She hears me. She breathes deeply. She hears me? Let us go further than us.

'If nothing has happened', says Ariane, 'before 25 July I will do it. Help me because I am going to help you.'

And the saying does. And the word *help* helps itself. And I give in to the force of the act-word.

25 July has the air of a coup d'état. It's not just that it is a speech act. It's that I believe. I believe that the 'will do' will be. I do not doubt. I tremble. It's already done. History ended on 25 July. That Ariane *gave* a date is a high theological act. Time goes into reverse and descends toward me, since 29 June, date of Ariane's speech it is already 25 July. This throws me into a sacred trance. I can no longer push back 25 July.

And the future is bearing down on us hard, its great moon occupies the centre of the sky and nothing dislodges it. The sun comes and goes without the moon giving in. I admire that Ariane dared to prophesy exactly. I will never forget this 25 July of 29 June. Or this 29 June that knew exactly which day the messiah would come. And already 25 July was tomorrow.

–I am miserable at not being able. –It is going to pass quickly, says Ariane. –I am closed up in the prison of without-saying, since my mother lost speech or else since she has not said anything more, in a language in silence. Then a great angel with solid wings beats the air above me.

And Ariane says. She says-does. And it is.

And the equivocation runs away like a ghost in the garden.

'Stand up straight!' When I find this injunction from another time in
Time Regained (page 247), on 30 July 2013, I am very surprised. It takes
me back right away to Oran, thus in 1943, to happiness, overseen by the
innocent dream of Omi my German grandmother and Ève, and I hear this
chirping of an imperative thrush that scanned every day of my childhood.
Stand up straight, sings the low melodious voice of my mother, *Halt'
dich grade!* alternates the high pitch of Omi, and it's a whole world that
appears to me, a Europe era that was foundering with its joyous and
hygienic ambitions of physical and therefore moral presence. I say 'Stand-
up-straight' and I see my mother coming toward my unleashed passion,
young svelte and military, the uprightness and composure of her step that
nothing frightens, and her smile that, as soon as I managed to glimpse it,
closed up again the abysses that terrified me. This Standupstraight had
meanings that my mothers did not suspect but incarnated. According to
my mother it was an antitubercular attitude and the principle of natural
elegance. But I divined upon seeing these two rather small women erect
themselves the idea of dignity and courage that animated them. Adroit,
solid, agile, indefatigable, Ève does her whole life on foot, backpack,
at most taking the bus to get across cities, certain of her body cut out
straight, no curves, neither hips nor buttocks, full of regrets upon seeing
her daughter bent over a plank all day with a devil on her shoulder. From
this rigorous splendour there remained a supple ruin that was changed in
January 2013 into a rusted rigidity. She cried out when she had to fold her
carcass to sit down on the toilet-chair and often we gave up, vanquished
by her iron resistance. As if her uprightness had petrified.

I say to myself 'Standupstraight' and I hear my mother's hope, which
I disappointed by answering her combative calculations with the unlimited primacy of writing. I have always been bent over in the tower that
she was.

Everything is in the tone. Thus when I say: 'I am unhappy' that can be
understood in various ways, according to the height of my voice

When Ève says: 'I am unhappy', it's altogether different. It means: I
have ceased being happy, my happiness is past I was young and strong
a long time ago, life is far away. When Ariane say: 'it's going to pass
quickly', still something else. Ariane thunders. Wonders. Concerning the
word *wonder*, as well. When I give it to Ève to read she says: '*Wonder*
is thunder.' She no longer reads. She no longer sets the tone. *Wondering*
stopped in spring 2012. She had no tone left. All summer 2012 I would
put books in her hands, they said nothing to her. Among them, silence.
However her hands wanted to *hold* the volume firmly. Ève holds onto
books like a man at sea.

'*Je vais le faire!*' 'I am going to do it!' says Ariane, and I clearly hear the homophony of *faire* with *fer*, iron. It's as if I had heard Ariane say to me: stand-up-straight, come out of your mother. Or: hold tight onto your crown. Eat! And also a good piece of meat. Powerful mystery of messages that circulate by telepathic channels: through Ariane's voice the same orders that my mother gave me come back to me from the very distant time when she was strength and I was her worry. It's like when my mother took control of my operations. 'My dear Hélène,' she would write, 'it seems to me that you are going to be done with the marvellous J. I point out to you that I had the same work done as you by the painter for only 500 – with a lot of handiwork. When one is not rolling in money, you have to get informed. You paid the highest price for mediocre work everywhere. We are wonderfully set up on the seventh floor of the Rue d'Isly now Ben Mehidi Larbi with a view you will love.' She preceded me toward the exit. A long time ago now.

'I am going to lend you a hand.' This voice, in me, this firm hand, all of a sudden I thought I recognised it! But it's the voice of Reason! I say to myself ecstatically. The voice of my mother. –You have borne more than 9999% of what people bear, says Ariane. It's inhuman and it brings no returns. It's all her.

–But how does one do it? says my voice of weakness and flight. –You give tranquillisers. You crush them up, says my mother. It's what I should have done and not said for Omi. –But why didn't you do it, dearest Maman? –I was afraid of being relieved. You were not there. I couldn't talk to you about it. Unfortunately Omi had been very bored for years and her boredom prevented me from finding a husband. Unfortunately you didn't help me, and I never had the chance to begin thinking what I thought. Finally Omi said: do it. And I didn't do it.

–Your mother has beautiful hair. I am not afraid to say so, says Ariane. Ève has a good hairdresser. For the rest she's a broken woman.

The voice of Victoire comes joyously out of the sea where my mother young Ève liked to swim with her sister. Merely eighty-five years have passed. The same brief duration that stretches between Proust's sorrow and mine. I say to the young Victoire: I am sad, worried sick. Ève is sad in me, worried sick. Double sad worry. –In case of double sadness, take or give three Lamaline per day of worry alternating with Xanax. Without hesitating. Without alternating hesitation. Don't hesitate. Give. How the sea excites one. The voice of Victoire evolves with the mystifying grace of a lark whose song one moment bursts invisible from the sky the next moment from the earth.

On 29 June I was no longer making any distinction between one reality and a reality other. All of space was but one epic time where I saw move away and melt into the fog of my thinking many Èves each sounding so different.

–She will soon have no more hair, says the nurse with violet eyes. This idea affects me violently. Thus we are going toward the inhuman piece by piece.

–When did she become my baby? I asked Anne, this ravishing morning of golden lights of 15 August. –In 2006, says my daughter. I'm a materialist, says my daughter. I remember. –I erase, I hesitate.

Oh angels of Osnabrück, Strasbourg and Oran come and take Maman. Let me feed on my tears.

But just as Maman was on the way for years before the departure, so she might be in the process of coming back to me from the faraway unknown country where successive illnesses and weaknesses had banished her.

According to my daughter she had become another, this wholly other, after her pneumonia, which was eight years ago, she lost then her principal features, agility, balance, rapidity, she was dead and she resuscitated on the other side, old, tottering, invalid, completely the opposite of Ève but I had not registered this metamorphosis, I still saw her in my mind in love with the Ève from before, go out in the morning to the market where she had stopped going for eight years but where she went mentally, the only warning that reached me came from the bathroom in Arcachon, by which one could measure my mother's decline. I could not deny the reduction by degree. In 2006 Ève stood in my bedroom next to the bathroom, an old naked nymph whose back was devoured by pustules of pemphigoid, I rubbed her with the cortisone that was killing her to treat her with an incalculable slowness, and that at length flayed her alive. What was keeping her alive led her to her ruin, her existence was unfolding under the double law of the *pharmakon*, the good does a good deal of evil, and me too I was pushing her out of a pharmakonic love to push back her limits. In 2010 she climbed in stages. At the landing she would rest for ten minutes. Then we continued up. The climb would take half an hour. In 2012, we no longer climbed, barely could we cover three metres. The shower went out of her world. I sat her on a chair in the kitchen and splashed her from a bowl. One by one we give our goods back to fate. We had lost the world on high. My mother on the upper storey was no longer. She no longer entered.

–She was happy, says my daughter. Finally the right to childhood and maternal solicitude, after ninety-nine years, one is allowed to rest from the pitfalls of the world. Now she had only death to combat.

–I am well treated. People take care of me. They give me my choco-
lates to eat. No one beats me. She was laughing on the telephone.

–It's as if I had a child, the most childish of children and the most feeble,
and the child was beaten. I wanted to say this to Victoire, on 29 June.

–I am going to do it, says Ariane.

–We stop, says Victoire.

And I meditated on the opposite mysteries. Do not give in order to
give. Stop giving life to death.

My mother, who until the age of ninety-nine had helped me, had
become my child, from one day to the next she had put maternity into
my hands and I had said yes. It's from the suffering of the child who is
most a child of all the children, the most dependent, the most wounded,
that I was suffering now. And when I needed my mother, she was no
longer able to return to the solicitude that had been my strength and my
peace. –Sort things out yourself, the good times are over, says Ève to me.
–I miss her, I say to my daughter, I miss my mother, and for years. She
left me in her place a poor old damaged baby. I say, on 29 July.

I forget. I remember: I say to my daughter: –Help me. This time I give.
–You can count on me. Solid with the solidity of my mother, authentic
daughter of Ève, harder than me, resolved for a long time, she has the
big calming smile of Maman. –What day is it? I asked, for there were
no more days in the fog. –Sunday. –That'sgood! said my mother's voice
of silence. Ève is sleeping, trembling. Behind her, still there while she is
no longer there, less than Ève, less like her than her dresses and her big
Mephisto sandals that trail years behind her last blouse, burned to a
cinder, only the eyes are safe but she opens them for only a second every
other day, her fingers crushed with bruises. As if I had seen Kronos chew
her up. I desire her. I lean over her face that Pity has left for my enjoyment. I kiss passionately the hole where her mouth was. It is Sunday.
Maman, I say into the hole. 30 June.

You have forgotten, the notebook tells me. I am consulting it on 22
August. The horror of seeing her in this state of ruined fortress, the awful
splendour of a life stronger than herself. Ève is growing. I venerate her.

The frequency of the word *awful* during these frontier days.

Marvellous children. They too are growing. Seeds of Ève.

Seeds of Ève title of the book, the notebook says to me.

On 29 June you are sitting beside Ève, the notebook recalls. You do
not know that this Saturday is the last Saturday of your history but each

of your gestures depicts premonition. You are taking these notes at her bedside in a little book. I am in the room next door, but something that has no name prevents you from coming to get me, holds you back in a mystical adhesion to the edge of Ève.

She is half-sleeping her eyes half-open, visor lowered, issues some untranslatable *ah! ah! ah!* I respond: my darling love, mydear, my old demolished goddess. She nods her head. I translate: I hear you. I ran out of the projection of our film, I tell her, a fear and a need hastened me toward you, I write to her. I speak to her with every means, I sing to her in languages of smiles and invocations, in every direction, I beat my heart on her brain, she hears me with her forehead, with her neck, with everything that still moves and lives,

nods   nods

Oh angels of Osnabrück come get Ève when you can

Ève is breathing heavily: the little book joins Lamaline and Xanax humble servants of our last act, I am aware of that. Here everything is hurried, succinct, telegraphic, abridged. Little neurological tic of the jaw that's trying to eat Maman's tongue calms down. She is perfectly conscious. She uses her ultimate muscles, her whole voice is in her neck.

Nods   Nods

After a long trail that was shadowy, twisted, haunted with sins, grave accusations, scaldings of betrayals, I arrive it seems to me at a roundabout where I find Ève again and the rosy radiance of her good sense

–I remark, she says, it seems to me, that there is no sense any longer in remaining like this in double suffering. The papers are in the little red briefcase. I have prepared for you addressed envelopes for all the organisations to send with my death announcement. Don't let yourself be cheated by the funeral home, check the estimate and the bill. Also notify the office of the mayor of Osnabrück, that I didn't make the envelope. –What do I do for the minimumrabbi? –Your son will have an idea. I think he has a yarmulke. –Anne too? –Nods. –Anne thinks that there has to be all the same a small announcement in the newspapers? –Don'tgiveadamn. I don't read those things.

Breathing badly. I pulverise water. Her whole face is cracks. Crack of the eye, crack of the mouth. I cover with kisses her crack of a mouth, her hollow cheeks, her silent forehead.

Saturday 29 Lamaline 6.30 in the evening – Sunday 30 Lamaline 9 o'clock in the morning, Xanax 2 o'clock in the afternoon; Xanax 6 o'clock in the evening, Xanax 11 o'clock at night. I notice that I'm keeping the books in the spirit of Ève: precision is the poem, exactitude is morality. She returns from the Arcachon market, sits down on her sofa, notes in her notebook:

salmon fish 7.86 (29.40)
shrimp 9.47   oysters N3 14.80   petrol 23.32
2 lettuces 2   1 cucumber 1.50   courgettes 0.80
chicken 18
bread 2.50   Sunday 13 heat, Monday 14 walk Pèreire beach, mussels 1lb 4.20 Florence 4.00, 19 July walk *along* the sea, book Hél. 9, jam 4.30 Leader Price 11.73, gr. beans at 3.50, Monoprix lift 0.80.

I return with her on Tuesday, 12 August 2008: mussels 3.30, battery 1.0, ham fruit 5, Monoprix Always 4, fish 24, sardines 3, jam 4.30, 6 eggs 1.20, petrol 23 litres 23.10, lift 0.80

This is a self-portrait. 'What have I been, who am I? I am going to be one hundred. Greater ones than I have died, she thought, I had her read *The Life of Henry Brulard*, that one didn't really know what he was doing, but he lived well. His Saint Bernard pass makes me think of Fred, he was ugly but very intelligent. After all I didn't occupy my life too badly, and now toolate. I was at the Sistine Chapel like a sheep, it's just like René, a good companion but no invention.

MAINTENANCE ÈVE, title of the book. In two hundred years one will be able to reconstitute the Life of Ève Klein down to the very penny.

I take the lift. It's going down.

I come back *to the writing*, that is to say, to the notebook with Ève Sunday, 30 June, at 6 o'clock in the morning, it's because the level of double suffering is so high that my whole being cries out for the remedy. Until 30 June this notebook was a handkerchief. I was wiping my tears. I was soaking up the blood. This morning I do not go to the notebook, for the first time I come out of it and I go back to it. I have questions to ask it. Who is Thewriting? The faithful one? My faithful ones. My daughters of her? Beware of her. [*Mes fidèles. Mes filles d'elle? Méfie d'elle*]. Or a paper Lamaline?

I reread this notebook, three hundred sorrows in thirty pages, to *discover* what it knows and what I did not know.

A thought: perhaps during this farewell-year, Thewriting toiled away, busied itself, as in Ève's Childbirthwithoutpain, in secret expectation, to prepare me in the method for the coming desert.

Forces and mysteries of the white notebook: it presents itself as a storehouse of *memory* external to me while I am full of forgetting, I have forgotten *everything*. Already I am *remaking* bandage-versions in which

I *believe*, substitute 'memories', already I am beginning to bear false witness, I felt it yesterday when with my sober and certain daughter we were evoking the years of the last six months, Anne, detaching herself, distinct, decided, from my ectoplasm, me remaking a form, pulling from my ashes a story, telling her: 'I have always thought like you,' and believing it. Making of a false truth a truth of consolation.

I was saying then: perhaps the book that I have to write, the fire-wall, the next field of wheat, the collection of wounds, has already been written by Thewriting, the commiserating one, so as to insure me against the famine that looms this summer? Perhaps Ève has prepared the picnic? And this book is full of her splendours and recipes.

When I wake her on 22 August in the morning my daughter murmurs: *Maman.* The word seeks me out. I am groping in the darkness where I see only her voice without timbre. Thus the word is not dead. The words of need want to live, especially that one. As I am in the fog of the bedroom, me too I murmur: *Maman,* and Ève's silence nods its head.

To ruminate: that help does not come from where and from whom one expects it. Doesn't come. Comes. An almost joyous gratitude toward all the forms of Help that stand guard around us, my friends my children the knights of these latter times (I don't use the word day there is no more day) honourable, discreet, firm, peaceful. Ariane enters like a great theatrical archangel, all sails deployed, come from our hero Jean Salvatore to respond to the distress call. Victoire pours sea water for me to drink. Each one 'plays her role' and it's as if the spirit of the young Ève had filled the room.

Three times she cried out a great cry, I don't know what the cry said, it was in Sunday's fog. A single sound. *AH!* I don't know and I know.

At noon I give her, with difficulty, something to drink. I use the syringe I insert the point in the crack. She doesn't swallow. She swallows. She raises her eyelids and murmurs, clearly, Hélène, Hélène. I say I adore you my great love. I turn the knife in the crack of my heart. I do not say: Ève, rise up and live. I lie down in her boat. I put my mouth on the crack of her soul and I suck the breath of my mother. Everything she has given me every day: every day.

–Don't forget my thought, as light as a shadow, on Sunday afternoon: 'it's the last *caca*'. A well-formed stool. But I cannot keep that. –I write all of this in the notebook. And the notebook keeps it. I cannot keep Ève's last *caca*. This is a moment of admiration: you never saw anyone keep more regular accounts. She knew and appreciated the word 'exonerate' and its double meaning, faecal and fiscal.

Monday, 1 July, 8 o'clock in the morning – Roro and I. It's time to change the nappy. She is calm. I could believe it, she was resting. A thread of light passed between her eyelids. I saw it, and looked, and I cried out: are you dead, Maman? and someone exclaimed she's dead? it was me and it was not me, in my chest, my heart yelled: Maman! Maman! As for me I felt right away that dead she would never be, it's the first time I see her deprived of the *strength* to make a sign, I had a searing pain for her, she was trying to raise her head, and the body couldn't any longer, surely she wanted to make a little effort and she was held back by a crushing fatigue and Roro cried mylit'l darling and she thought shesmine I thin of her alway do Franch or do Portugál Idore very much and she jumped with one leap over my prostrate body and I don't know how she took Ève's head and she wedged it between her two big tits and then I covered her entirely with a fabric of kisses finally I could kiss her everywhere without her screaming with pain, it had been months that I had had this miserable hunger, I painted her whole envelope of spotted skin with very light touches from my tongue, I scattered an avid, immense love it's the first time I can, I hurry, eternity is so brief and we feel that time is going to enter with its heavy and brutal step in five minutes and separate us from Maman, Roro and I are on her body like piglets, I crawl beneath the sheet, I am writing this with eyes closed to begin again to feel myself caressing her while skimming with my fingers, which alas wound her without her knowing it, the surfaces of her body that the bandages spared, her belly, the top of her thighs, her ankles. She smells good. I love her carnally, with delicacy, the word Maman reigns, I form one body with my childhood earth, with Maman my native city. Monday bears down on me like a mountain on the march, it is petrified Birnam Wood, a wall of trees seized in their sleep. I am trembling, I feel my strength draining, my weakness mounting. It's Maman who is flowing out of me. I exsanguinate.

Last pages of our life, notes the notebook. I want to keep it set it down without losing it

On 14 July in Arcachon I take up again 1 July, one more time, one more time, I am seeking, I am seeking, it is 8 o'clock, she has departed, she has just departed, she is there, she is in the train, the train is there, I am on the platform imperceptibly the train 'lifted off', I don't know at which second, the separation happened, the separation does not happen, it happens only in our absence. I was there and I was not there. I don't know when she went out. She left her body in her place. She had the habit of not moving a centimetre for ten hours, at dawn I found her in the *exact* position where I had left her sleeping at dusk and revisited at 11 o'clock at night. When I had gone to see her at 5 o'clock in the morning on Monday she was just as I had left her six hours earlier, after having injected some water, and like the other mornings, she was breathing in a discreet and regular way, I leaned over gently toward the verdict since her immobility was so absolute it was impossible to decide if she was where she was, if not in the greatest proximity, I leaned over my silence to her silence and was careful not to wake her for a vain and painful awakening since I would have deprived her of the shelter of rest without having anything better to offer her than the next torment with a medication, next I stayed in front of the computer, that is, four metres away from her, and she remained in silence behind my back and it's perhaps at one of the moments of this borderless and featureless time that a breath did not come to follow the following breath, the last second is lost among diverse seconds, she perhaps passed before me or behind me

she did not call me, she herself was perhaps not there the nonevent of nonève perhaps took place while she was sleeping, it perhaps escaped her, perhaps even nothing happened, it is perhaps nothing that came and thus I lost this very long unitive life at the corner of a time without minute.

Ève Cixous and Hélène Cixous

26 August 2013 at 5 o'clock in the morning
in the house in Arcachon

Ma grande Chérie

Tu es notre guide qui trône au-dessus de nous (au 1 é tage) et nous indique la route du succès. Bonheur. Prenez 2 chats et suivez leur itinéraire à travers vent et soleil. Heureusement qu'il y a Eve qui nous invite à l'immobilisation sans vent et soleil et qui ne refuse pas un bon café au lait, à bon entendeur salut!

quand je demande à maman de m'écrire une lettre, elle l'accomplit sans hésitation. Elle n'a jamais été aussi libre.

16.7.10